# Criminal Law

## Outlines, Diagrams, Exam Study Sheets

VisuaLaw Study Guide Volume 2

Duncan Brown and Jessica Patel

SULIS
ACADEMIC
PRESS

An imprint of Sulis International

Los Angeles | London

VisuaLaw Study Guides are based on the University of London Study Guide for Criminal Law. This publication is an independent work and is not connected with nor endorsed by the University.

Published by Sulis Academic Press
An imprint of Sulis International
www.sulisinternational.com



Front cover: "Old Bailey" in The Microcosm of London or London in Miniature, Volume II, London: Methuen and Company, Plate 58.

ISBN: 978-1-946849-00-7
Third Edition: February 2017

1. Law 2. Criminal

# Criminal Law

## Outlines, Diagrams, Exam Study Sheets

# Table of Contents

# Preface

This book contains three sections of material: Outlines, Diagrams, and Crib Sheets.

**Outlines** are detailed outlines of the course material, arranged by topic, including statutes, cases, and key terms, arranged for aid in studying, memorizing, and revising/reviewing.

**Diagrams** are perfect companions to the Course Outlines. These contain flow charts, diagrams, and other visual aids for each topic.

**Exam Study Sheets** are condensed outlines, based on the Course Outlines above. Perfect for "getting the big picture," for revising, and for testing yourself on the details. Each "crib sheet" contains 1–5 pages on each of the topics, including key statutes and cases.

These Study Guides are not intended as a substitute for required readings or any other assignments. Everything you need to know to pass the exams is not included here—this book is an outline of the subject and a companion study tool. If you understand and can discuss each element on each page, you will be well on your way to understanding the subject.

Send questions, errata, and suggestions to legal.yankee@sulisinc.com. Your input will help us continue to update and refine these study guides.

# Course Outlines

# 1. Introduction

These Outlines present the topics and subtopics of the course in standard outline form, along with key terms, cases, and statutes. Suggested study plan:

1. Look over the chapter which corresponds to the chapter you are about to study for your course.
2. Read your assigned readings and do any assigned activities. Peridically review the material in this Study Guide to reinforce the material.
3. Review the VisuaLaw Course Outline. Test yourself: are you able to discuss each item in detail? Go back over your reading material to strengthen the areas in which you are weak. Repeat until you have mastered the topic.
4. Repeat for each subject in the course.

When you are preparing for your exams, use the VisuaLaw Course Outlines to review the material you need to know, and guide you back to your course textbook and readings for information you need to review.

# 2. Elements of an Offense

## 2.1. General Analysis

### 2.1.1. Prosecution must prove BRD

### 2.1.2. Statutory offenses (e.g., Theft Act 1968), common law offenses (e.g., murder, manslaughter)

- Actus reus (External element)
    - Conduct
    - Circumstances
    - Consequences (if a result crime)
- Mens rea
    - Intention (specific intent)
    - negligence (basic intent)
    - recklessness (basic intent)
    - Internal element of crime
    - Must prove that, at the time, D had relevant state of mind
    - Mens rea must coincide with actus reus
    - Not always necessary for crime (strict liability)

## 2.2. Important: Limitations of the terms

### 2.2.1. "term of art" – technical term which has special significance

### 2.2.2. conventional terms, but mean nothing on their own

## 2.3. Proof of ingredients of an offense

### 2.3.1. Burden on prosecution to prove BRD

1. (see *Woolmington v DPP* (1935) AC 462)
2. Therefore, if offense is basic intent, must prove all elements of actus reus, regardless of how guilty his mind is (mens rea). See *Deller* (1952) 36 Cr. App. R. 184 2.3.2. Example: Criminal Damage Act 1971
3. Actus reus: "destroys or damages any property belonging to another" (conduct)
4. "without lawful excuse" (circumstances)
5. Property damaged (result)
6. If all of the above are proved, then actus reus is proved.
7. Must now also establish mens rea

    7.1 "intent" or "recklessness as to..."

## 2.4. Lawful Excuse

2.4.1. If D knew it was lawful, no mens rea

2.4.2. If D believed it was lawful, no mens rea.

2.4.3. If D believed it was not, but it was lawful: criminal liability negated

2.4.4. If D was not aware, but did have lawful excuse: he still had mens rea

2.4.5. Could argue that lawful excuse is not an element of offense, but a defense. See *Dadson* (1850) 175 E.R. 499.

## TABLE OF AUTHORITIES

**CASES**
*Dadson* (1850)
*Deller* (1952)
*Woolmington v DPP* (1935)

**STATUTES**
Criminal Damage Act 1971
Theft Act 1968

**TERMS**
Actus reus
basic intent
Lawful Excuse
Mens rea
result crime

# 3. Actus Reus: Voluntariness

## 3.1. Background

### 3.1.1. BOP on Pros to show that D was guilty BRD with a voluntary act. (*Woolmington v DPP* [1935] AC 462).

### 3.1.2. No act punishable if done involuntarily: without any control of mind: spasm, reflex action, concussion, sleepwalking. (*Bratty v Attorney-General for Northern Ireland* [1961] 3 All ER 523.

- Swarm of bees, malevolent passenger, blackout, vehicle failure (*Bell* (1985) R.T.R. 202).

## 3.2. Automatism is Complete defense (D not to blame at all)

### 3.2.1. Hypoglycaemia, concussion, alcohol, drugs

## 3.3. Limitations

### 3.3.1. Had some control

1. Any control, trance-like state, purposive movements
2. *A-G's Reference (No. 2 of 1992)* [1993]) 99 Cr App R
3. Draft Code less harsh (Law Com No. 177 Cl.33)

### 3.3.2. Insanity (Insane Automatism)

1. an internal factor and was therefore likely to recur.
2. Need not have suffered from it for any length of time
3. "Not guilty by reason of insanity" - special verdict, e.g. hospital order, mental hospital (mandatory until Criminal Procedure (Insanity and Unfitness to Plead) Act 1991 gave other options)

3.1 Raised by D: BOP to prove (*Woolmington*) — rare

3.2 Raised by P: BOP BRD (often raised in response to D's defense of sane automatism) 1) P must then prove by M'Naghten Rules (*M'Naghten's Case* (1843) 10 Cl & Fin 200.

3.3 Disease of the mind: hyperglycaemia, sleepwalking and epilepsy

## 3.4. Prior fault

### 3.4.1. Non-self-induced automatism

1. voluntary intoxication by alcohol or dangerous drugs
2. defence may not be relied upon where the offence is one of basic intent
3. taking non dangerous drugs may provide a defence to basic intent offences. (awareness of risk necessary?)

   3.1 Valium, committed arson (*Hardie* [1985] 1 WLR 64)

   3.2 Sufficient food after insulin (*Bailey* [1983] 1 WLR 760)

## TABLE OF AUTHORITIES

**CASES**
*A-G's Reference (No. 2 of 1992)* [1993])
*Bailey* [1983]
*Bell* (1985)
*Bratty v Attorney-General for Northern Ireland* [1961]
*Hardie* [1985]
*M'Naghten's Case* (1843)
*Woolmington v DPP* [1935]

**STATUTES**
Criminal Procedure (Insanity and Unfitness to Plead) Act 1991

**TERMS**
Insane Automatism

M'Naghten Rules
sane automatism

# 4. Actus Reus: Omissions

## Liability for Omission to Act

4.1.1. Sometimes a statute will state the actus reus is committed by omission (ex: willfully neglect a child: Children and Young Persons Act 1933 s 1(1))

4.1.2. Rarely found in common law

4.1.3. If an offense can be committed by omossion, then there must be a duty of care imposed on a particular class of people.

4.1.4. If a result crime, court must determine whether the omission might result in criminal activity

4.1.5. If D is found to have a duty of care, prosecution has burden to prove all other ingredients

4.1.6. Is an offense capable of being committed by omission?

- Murder (*Gibbins and Proctor* [1918] 13 CAR 134); manslaughter
- Not assault, though (*Fagan v MPC* [1969])

4.1.7. Was the Defendant Under a Duty to Act?

- Duty is not onerous
  - Not expected to put own life at risk
  - Reasonable standard (objective) – *Stone and Dobinson* (1977) 1 QB 345
- Difference between moral duty to act and legal duty to act (*Instan* (1893))
- Scope of duty unclear
  - Parent under legal duty to child, what about siblings? Neighbors?

- Supplier of illicit drugs? – *Evans* [2009] EWCA Crim 650, *Khan and Khan* (1994)

– Likely to depend on situation; scope of duties on closed

## 4.2. Duty to Act Under Common Law

4.2.1. *Pittwood* (1902) 19 TLR 37 -

4.2.2. *Miller* [1983] 2 AC 161 HL – AR can be a failure to act if D was cause

4.2.3. *Gibbins and Proctor* [1918] 13 Cr. App. R. 134 – context and acceptance and create a duty of care where one would not exist otherwise.

4.2.4. *Stone and Dobinson* [1977] 1 QB 345 – had duty of care because they took her into home and assumed it.

## 4.3. Distinguishing between an Act and an Omission

4.3.1. *Airedale NHS Trust v Bland* [1993] – omission, medical treatment.

4.3.2. *Re: A (Conjoined Twins: Surgical Separation)* [2001] – act, medical treatment

4.3.3. *R v Cox* [1992] – lethal injection

## 4.4. New Categories of Duty

4.4.1. *Khan and Khan* [1994] – suppliers of drug, no duty to call for medical care

4.4.2. *Singh (Gurphal)* [1999] – is duty a matter of law or matter of fact

4.4.3. *Willoughby* [2004] – duty of care question usually for jury.

4.4.4. *Evans* [2009] – gave heroin to sister, she self-administered, dead in the morning. Convicted of manslaughter, appealed, arguing the judge was wrong to leave it to jury. CA dismissed appeal: when a person is the one who created the situation, ought to have known possible results. Q of duty of care existence was for judge, not jury, but judge was just following *Willoughby*.

## 4.5. The 'Circumstances' element of actus reus.

4.5.1. Some crimes require the existence of specific circumstances as part of actus reus.

4.5.2. Ex: Criminal Damage Act 1971 s.1(1), what is destroyed must be 'property belonging to another.'

4.5.3. State of Affairs as Actus Reus

- Sometimes a 'state of affairs' or 'situation' is necessary, which sometimes results in strange and unfair results.
- Larsonneur *(1933) 24 Cr App* R *74*
- *Winzar v Chief Constable of Kent* (1983) The Times 28 March

# TABLE OF AUTHORITIES

**CASES**
*Airedale NHS Trust v Bland* [1993]
*Evans* [2009]
*Fagan v MPC* [1969]
*Gibbins and Proctor* [1918]
*Khan and Khan* (1994)
*Larsonneur* (1933)
*Miller* [1983]
*Pittwood* (1902)
R *v Cox* [1992]
*Re: A (Conjoined Twins: Surgical Separation)* [2001]
*Singh (Gurphal)* [1999]
*Stone and Dobinson* [1977]
*Willoughby* [2004]
*Winzar v Chief Constable of Kent* (1983)

**STATUTES**
Children and Young Persons Act 1933 s 1(1)
Criminal Damage Act 1971 s.1(1)

# 5. Actus Reus: Consequences

## 5.1. Causation and Liability

### 5.1.1. Usually self-evident

### 5.1.2. More complex when intervening events and actions of others affect the chain of events

### 5.1.3. Causation is considered element of the actus reus of result crimes

– but an argument can be made that the mens rea is a factor that could influence the outcome of a trial or appeal.

### 5.1.4. Conduct must be both the factual and the legal cause of the result (below)

## 5.2. Factual Causation

### 5.2.1. Determined by reference to the sine qua non

– This is a necessary condition, but not the only required condition

– Whether something is a factual cause of an event is a question of fact for the jury

– See *Carey* [2006] EWCA Crim 17.

### 5.2.2. Causation by omission

– Court assumes it can. See *Instan* (1893] 1 QB 450.

## 5.3. Legal Causation

5.3.1. Judge will direct jury as to whether something can be the legal cause, then jury decides whether not the facts suggest the particular situation was.

5.3.2. Expert evidence often plays a role in determining cause. It is not determinative, though

- *Jordan* [1956] 40 CAR 152 has been criticized on this grounds
- *Malcherek* [1981] 1 WLR 696 - did not overrule Jordan, but described it as "exceptional"
- Similarly, *Smith* [1959] 2 QB 35 described it as "very particular case depending upon its exact facts."
- Glanville Williams believes that words used to describe this second notion of cause, but thinks it is not so much a test of causation as moral reaction
- It is freq pleaded by Ds as a last ditch attempt to be exonerated from liability, when all other elements of AR and MR have been established
- Other terms: operating, substantial, substantive, significant

### 5.3.3. Operating and Substantial Cause

- But does not have to be the main cause
    - *Smith* [1959] 2 QB 35 – 'if at time of death the original wound is still an operating cause and substantial cause...putting it another way...only if the second cause is so overwhelming as to make the original wound merely part of the history...'
    - *Cato* [1976] 1 WLT 110 – the culpable act must be more than a minimal cause of the result: 'it was a cause outside the de minimis range, and effectively bearing upon the acceleration of the moment of the victim's death.'
- The result must be attributable to the culpable act
    - Dalloway (1847) 2 Cox 273

- *R v Campbell (Andre), R v Yateman (Jermaine), R v Henry (Lloyd Rudolf)* [2009] EQCA Crim 50
- Victims must be taken as found
- *Blaue* [1975] 1 WLR 1411.

## 5.4. Intervening causes

### 5.4.1. Once a D starts a chain of events, he is liable unless it is broke by some novus actus interveniens: act of third party, act of V, or act of God/nature.

- Where it was not reasonably foreseeable
- Operated to render the defendants original conduct no longer an operating and substantial cause, just part o the background history.

### 5.4.2. *Pagett* [1983] 76 Cr App R 279

### 5.4.3. Escape Clause

- Where D frightens V so much that the V kills or injures self trying to escape, as long as the reaction is not so 'daft' as to make it V's own act, it will not break chain of causation - *William and Davis* [1992] 1 WLR 380 – jury to bear in mind the particular characteristic of the victim; how V might act without thought and deliberation.

### 5.4.4. Killing by Fright

- *Hayward* (1908) 21 Cox 692 – abnormal state of V's health does not affect question of whether D knew of it, if it proved to jury than the death was accelerated by D's unlawful act
- *Watson* [1989] 2 All ER 865 – D burgled house of frail 87-year-old, verbally abused him when he awoke; V had heart attack and died. Appealed. HELD: jury can decide if that is what caused V's death.

### 5.4.5. Neglect by the Victim

- Where V neglects to treat an injury inflicted by D and death results, D will likely be held responsible.

- *Dear* [1996] Crim LR 595 – D attacked V with Stanley knife, V having sexually abused D's daughter. V's wounds were stitched, reopened, V did not obtain medical help, bled to death. HELD: not helpful to require juries to embark on analysis whether V was negligent or grossly negligent (one would break chain, other would not)

– Medical Interventions

- *Jordan* [1965] – D not held responsible for stabbing of V, because V received 'palpably wrong' medical treatment when wounds had almost healed. [but *Smith* [1959] isolated *Jordan* by saying it was a 'very particular case depending on its own facts' – did not overrule though].

- *Malcherek* [1981] – 'there may be occasions, although they will be rare, when the original injury has ceased to operate as a cause at all, but in the ordinary case if the treatment is given bona fide by competent...evidence will not be admissible to show that treatment would not have been administered in the same way by other medical practitioners...'

- *Cheshire* [1991] – negligent medical treatment could only break chain where it was so independent of D's acts; in itself so potent in causing death, that it makes D's acts insignificant.

### 5.4.6. Acts of God/Nature

– Generally these are deemed not to have been reasonably foreseeable

– Unlawful Administration of Controlled Drugs

## TABLE OF AUTHORITIES

**CASES**
*Blaue* [1975]
*Carey* [2006]
*Cato* [1976]
*Cheshire* [1991]
*Dalloway* (1847)

*Dear* [1996]
*Hayward* (1908)
*Instan* (1893]
*Jordan* [1956]
*Malcherek* [1981]
*Pagett* [1983]
R *v Campbell (Andre),* R *v Yateman (Jermaine),* R *v Henry (Lloyd Rudolf)* [2009]
*Smith* [1959]
*Watson* [1989]
*William and Davis* [1992]

**TERMS**
novus actus interveniens
sine qua non

# 6. Mens Rea

## 6.1. Intro

### 6.1.1. Overview

– Most serious offenses require MR

– A legal term, not a term of morality or ethics (has not always been the case, though)

– actus non facit reum, nisi mens sit rea

  • Does not apply to crimes of negligence or strict liability

– Motive is generally irrelevant in criminal law; *Chandler v DPP* [1964] AC 763

  • Ex: a doctor who does a mercy killing is still guilty of murder

  • But...if primary purpose is to relive pain, but knows it will hasten death, does not have mens rea; *Adams* [1957] Crim LR 365; *Airdale NHS Trust v Bland* [1993] 2 WLR 316

  • Difference between allowing to die and killing

    • mistaken belief may negate the D's mens rea

### 6.1.2. Basic Intent

– Recklessness is sufficient

– P prove BRD that D was reckless (ware of risk, R v G [2004]

– Self-intoxication not a relevant defense

### 6.1.3. Specific Intent

– Ex: murder (intention to kill or to cause GBH; *Vickers* [1957] 2 QB 664; *Moloney* [1985]

- P must proof intent; recklessness will not suffice for such a crime
  1) i.e.; reckeless is insufficient for murder (specific intent crime) but is sufficient for manslaughter (basic intent crime)
- Self-intoxication defense is relevant defense

#### 6.1.4. Ulterior intent

- If D commits one crime while intending to commit another, he is guilty of both the basic mens rea (recklessness or intent of the first) and an ulterior intent of the second (even if he does not actually commit it)
- Examples
  - Burglary: enters building as a trespasser with intent to commit other crime(s)
  - Wounding with intent to cause GBH
  - Wounding or causing GBH with intent to resist/prevent arrest

### 6.2. Intention

#### 6.2.1. More blameworthy than recklessness, deserves more punishment

#### 6.2.2. Direct intent = purpose to achieve particular result

#### 6.2.3. Oblique intent = (a level of risk-taking that it almost indistinguishable from intentional wrong-doing)particular result is not primary purpose, he should know that result will happen because of his actions

- D puts bomb on a plane because he wants to collect insurance money. Does not want to kill anyone, hopes they survive. Blows up plane in flight. Intent: destroy plane, not kill people; oblique intent: murder *a. Important cases (has been contentious issue) — all important ones concern murder*

- Cases such as *DPP v Smith* [1961] AC 290 and *Hyam* [1975] used test which went beyond ordinary meaning of word 'intention' (many disagreed with *Hyam*, that it blurred distinction. Not overruled, but no longer followed:
- *Moloney* [1985] - was death/GBH a natural consequence of D's voluntary act and; did D foresee hat consequences as natural consequence of his act?
- HL further defined these guidelines in *Hancock and Shankland*; further refined in *Nedrick* [1986]
  i) jury to be directed that they cannot infer intention unless death/GBH was virtual certainty as result of D's actions (not MUST FIND, but ENTITLED to find)
- *Woolin* [1998] 3 WLR 382 HL
    - judge blurred the line between intention and recklessness (departed from *Woolin*) thus between murder and manslaughter
    - Issue arose: Lord Steyn's substituion of 'find' for 'infer' — did this change 'foresight of virtual certainty' from evidence the jruy may infer D intended consequence to substantive law that they must be satisified BRD that D foresaw the consequence as being reasonably certain
    - Issue arose: IS the direction of general application or only for murder?
        - *Walker v Hayles* (1990) 90 CR App R 226 adopted Nedrick direction in case of attempt, but blurred the line between INT and RECK using 'very high degree of probability)
- Matthews and Alleyne *(2003)*

## 6.3. Recklessness

6.3.1. "unjustified risk-taking" (some risk-taking can be justified by context) ['maliciously' often seen in 19th century statutes, same as recklessness now]

6.3.2. Knowing that there is a risk that a consequence may result, he takes it anyway and it is unreasonable to do so (deliberate conscious risk-taking)

6.3.3. Debate: should liability and punishment for a crime of recklessness be imposed

- for advertant or subjective recklessness (punish because he was deliberately chosen to increase risk of) 1) Most crimes
- Inadvertent or objective recklessness (punish because
    - Criminal damage — *Caldwell* [1982] AC 341 — D could be reckless even if risk not foreseen (here applied to reckless driving, offense since repealed) — much criticism of rule
    - D did an act which created an obvious risk of damage
- When D did the act he either
    - did not give any thought to risk ('*Caldwell* recklessness')
    - knew there was a risk, but proceeded anyway
    - *Caldwell* Overruled by *R v G* [2003] (read this case)
        - Caldwell misinterpreted word 'reckless' in Act

6.3.4. Courts originally gave this a subjective meaning — *Cunningham* [1957] 2 QB 396

## 6.4. Coincidence of AR and MR

6.4.1. MR and AR of a crime must coincide in time (if crime requires MR) — *Jakeman* (1982) 76 Cr App R 223

6.4.2. If the AR can be a continuous activity, the MR must occur at some point during the AR — *Fagan v MPC* [1969]

6.4.3. Important Cases

- *Thabo Meli* (1954)
- *Church* (1966) — Similar facts, but no preconceived plan. Knocked unconscious, believed dead, threw in river, where V drowned.
- *Le Brun* (1991) — Fight, D hit V on jaw, knocked unconscious. D dragged her body away, but slipped and head hit pavement, fractured skull and died.
- *A-G's Reference (No. 4 of 1980)* (1981) — knocked V downstairs. Thinking she was dead, cut her body into pieces to dispose of her. Impossible to know which act caused death. (See S&H p130)

## 6.5. Transferred Malice

6.5.1. In doing an unlawful act with intent, if D commits another unlawful act, even if accident, D is guilty of second offense — *Latimer* (1889)

- If A intends to kill B, but kills C because he thought he was B, A guilty of murder.
- If A intends to break window of House A, but accidentally breaks window of House C, guilty of criminal damage
    - But not where AR achieved is not the AR intended
- If A shoots B but misses and breaks window of house, no guilty of criminal damage

6.5.2. Principle of transferred malice is relevant in respect of any of the defences available

- If A does/says something to B; B does something that is a 'qualifying trigger' under Coroners and Justice Act 2009 s55 and kills A, B may plead partial defense of loss of control under s.54
- If instead, B accidentally kills C while trying to kill A; may be charged with murder under transferred malice; B can still plead loss of control

## 6.6. Negligence

6.6.1. Not really a MR term, but spoke of that way

6.6.2. Assessed objectively: reasonable person

6.6.3. A person is unaware of the risk in question but ought to have been (expected of a reasonable person)

6.6.4. Very few offenses of negligence

- Gross negligence manslaughter — *Adomako* [1995] 1 AC 171 — ordinary principles of negligence apply where D has a duty of care towards V who died.
- Rape (lacks reasonable belief that V was consenting)

## 6.7. Strict Liability

6.7.1. An offense where (in one of more elements of AR) no MR or NEGL need be proved — *R v Lemon and Gay News Ltd* [1979] AC 617 HL

- Must still be a voluntary act

6.7.2. It is a question of statutory interpretation

6.7.3. Presumption of MR if statute is silent — *Sweet v Parsley* [1970] AC 133 HL; *B (a minor)* [2000] 2 WLR 452

- Statutory context of words: court may look at other provisions in the statute, but not definitive — *Sweet*
- Subject matter of the offense

- *Sherras v de Rutzen* [1895] — exceptions to presumption
- non criminal in any real sense
- public nuisances

– summary modes of enforcing civil rights

- 'Truly Criminal' — *Gammon v A-G of Hong Kong* (1985) - five principles to be considered when determining
- there is a presumption of law that mens rea is required before a person can be held guilty of a criminal offence;
- the presumption is particularly strong where the offence is "truly criminal" in character
- the presumption applies to statutory offences, and can be displaced only if this is clearly or by necessary implication the effect of the statute
- the only situation in which the presumption can be displaced is where the statute is concerned with an issue of social concern, and public safety is such an issue
- even where a statute is concerned with such an issue, the presumption of mens rea stands unless it can also be shown that the creation of strict liability will be effective to promote the objects of the statute by encouraging greater vigilance to prevent the commission of the prohibited act
    - *Cheshire County Council ex parte Helliwell* (1991)

# TABLE OF AUTHORITIES

**CASES**

*A-G's Reference (No. 4 of 1980)* (1981)
*Adams* [1957]
*Adomako* [1995]
*Airdale NHS Trust v Bland* [1993]
*B (a minor)* [2000]
*Caldwell* [1982]
*Chandler v DPP* [1964]

*Cheshire County Council ex parte Helliwell* (1991)
*Church* (1966)
*Cunningham* [1957]
*DPP v Smith* [1961]
*Fagan v MPC* [1969]
*Gammon v A-G of Hong Kong* (1985)
*Hancock and Shankland*
*Hyam* [1975]
*Jakeman* (1982)
*Le Brun* (1991)
*Matthews and Alleyne* (2003)
*Moloney* [1985]
*Nedrick* [1986]
R *v G* [2003]
R *v Lemon and Gay News Ltd* [1979]
*Sherras v de Rutzen* [1895]
*Sweet v Parsley* [1970]
*Thabo Meli* (1954)
*Vickers* [1957]
*Walker v Hayles* (1990)
*Woolin* [1998]

# 7. Unlawful Homicide: Murder and Manslaughter

## 7.1. Homicide in Context

## 7.2. Distinction between murder and manslaughter (both share a common actus reus)

### 7.2.1. Murder and Involuntary Manslaughter (defined by the mens rea differences)

- Constructive Manslaughter (Manslaughter by an unlawful and dangerous act)
  - unintentionally and unforeseeably kills another while committing an unlawful act which was likely to cause GBH
- Gross Negligent Manslaughter
  - breach of duty towards the deceased which caused the death, so serious as to warrant criminal liability
- Reckless Manslaughter
  - deliberately taking an unjustified risk of causing serious injury

### 7.2.2. Murder and Voluntary Manslaughter (difference is not of mens rea; but mitigating circumstances

- Loss of self-control
  - Coroner's and Justice Act 2009 s.54, 56 — replaced CL partial defences of provocation with new partial defence to murder
  - where killing resulted from loss of self-control through a 'qualifying trigger'

– diminished responsibility

- Homicide Act 1957 s.2 — at time of killing, suffering from diminished responsibility; replaced by new definition in Coroners and Justice Act 2009 s.52 (see CH 8)

– suicide pact

- Homicide Act 1957 s.4 —manslaughter not murder if acting in pursuance of a suicide pact

## 7.3. The Actus Reus of Murder and Manslaughter (written by Sir Edward Coke [1552-1634])

### 7.3.1. Unlawfully

– excludes such things as killing in self-defense with reasonable force

– *Re A (conjoined twins)* [2000] 4 All ER 961, Court of Appeal — operation to separate conjoined twins to save the life of the stronger was not unlawful

### 7.3.2. Killeth

– Action must be legal cause of death

– Only necessary to show the act(s) accelerated the death

- ) *Re A (children)* — operation would be legal cause of death, even though she would die anyway without the operation: the operation would legally kill her

– Medical definition of death considered in

- *R v Malcherek; R v Steel* [1981] 2 All ER 422 — victims of 2 attacks placed on life-support; Drs concluded they were brain dead, should be disconnected; Trial judge withdrew from jury issue of the cause of death because at time of death original injuries still operating as cause. On Appeal: Drs did not carry out all the tests necessary to determine brain death; jury should have been allowed to consider which was cause of death

- Death: 1) cessation of cardiopulmonary system; but due to medical technology that can keep a those functions going (2) irreversible cessation of the brain stem (so PVS is not legally dead)
- This definition was accepted by the HL in *Airdale NHS Trust v Bland* [1993] 1 All ER 821 7.3.3. *any reasonable creature in rerum natura* (a human life in being)
    - Not murder/manslaughter to kill fetus in womb, maybe be 'unlawfully procuring a miscarriage, though
        - Offenses Against the Person Act 1861; Infant Life (Preservation) Act 1929 s.1
        - fetus becomes a human being when
            - entire body of child emerged from mother
            - must be alive and have existence independent of mother
        - (murder requires intention to kill or cause GBH *of a human being)*
        - *Attorney General's Reference (No. 3 of 1994)* [1993] 1 AC 789 — only where original injuries were targeted against the fetus and not the mother than D may be convicted of murder. [D stabbed pregnant GF in back; no injury to fetus detected, but born prematurely and died 4 mos later attributed to premature birth; HL rejected argument that fetus could be part of mother - intention towards fetus not the same as intention towards mother; intent could not be transferred, either, because it would be a 'double' transfer (mother to fetus, fetus to child); but could be constructive manslaughter

### 7.3.4. Within the Queen's Peace

- Doesn't apply to killing of enemy in war (but killing of enemy in captivity is)

– Offences Against the Person Act 1861; British Nationality Act 1948 s.3 — murder/MS committed against a
Brit outside the UK can be tried/punished in England

### 7.3.5. within a year and a day

– used to be rule from 16th century

– 1994 Law Commission recommended abolition in light of modern medicine

– Law Reform (Year and A Day Rule) Act 1996, s.1

## 7.4. The mens rea of Murder

– *'malice aforethought' — misleading, modern formulation: intention to cause* GBH (*Moloney* [1985] AC 905)

#### 7.4.1. Meaning of Intention

- *Woollin* [1999] 1 CR App R 8; applied in *Matthews and Alleyne* [2003] 2 Cr App R 30
- If aim/purpose was to kill/GBH –intention
- If not aim/purpose, but knew that death?GBH was virtually certain, jury is 'entitled not obliged to find' intention
- IF D foresaw risk of death? GBH, but lower level than virtual certainty — not sufficient for intention

### 7.4.2. Intention to cause GBH

– *Vickers* [1957] 2 QB 664; *Cunningham* [1982] AC 566 — intention to cause GBH suffice for murder

– This aspect of mens rea caused considerable academic and judicial criticism — see *Powell and Daniels; English* [1999] 1 AC 1 — considered by many to be unjust

### 7.4.3. RECENT DEVELOPMENTS

– *Mount* [2010] EWCA Crim 2974 — M wanted to get back together with GF; concerned about her relationship with V; M at pub drinking; got knife ('to scare off') and went and met V; argument; V starts fight; M stabs him; no one knew he was mortally injured; died; convicted of murder; appealed on jury instructions: 'if jury did not think intent to kill/GBH was proved BRD; then MS' instruction led to jury convicting of murder; HELD: Instructions would not have led jury to convict of murder; conviction upheld

## 7.5. Involuntary Manslaughter

### 7.5.1. By Unlawful and Dangerous Act (Constructive Manslaughter)

- *constructive - liability for one crime rests of commission of less serious act*
- D performed an unlawful act
  - ) *Franklin* [1883] — civil wrong insufficient for constructive MS
  - *Andrews* [1937], HL — Negligence offense not sufficient, must be an offense that requires mens rea
  - ) *Lowe* [1973] — omission not sufficient
  - Most common — assault or battery,
    - but see *Goodfellow* [1986] — criminal damages sufficient
    - but see *Watson* [1989], CA — burglary contrary to Theft Act 1968 s.9(1)(a) might be sufficient
  - Prosecution prove all elements of crime
  - *Cato* [1967]; *DPP v Newbury* [1977] — imply conviction without proof of all elements of base crime
  - *Lamb* [1967] — better approach, D accidentally shot his friend
- Unlawful act was dangerous
  - *Church* [1966], CA — if 'all sober and reasonable people' would inevitably recognize that the unlawful act subjected V to risk of some harm albeit not serious

– unlawful act was legal cause of death

### 7.5.2. Manslaughter and the Administration of Drugs

– *Cato* (1976) — If D injects V and V dies, D guilty (even if drug prepared; injected with consent). Offenses Against the Person Act 1861 s.23

– *Dalby* (1982), CA — D supplied V with Diconal tablets (legal?); injected self back at home; died. HELD: act of supply itself was not directed at victim, did not cause direct injury

- But later decisions held that there is no need for unlawful acts to be aimed at V; *Dalby* explained that there was no causal link between supply and death. *Mitchell* [1983]; *Goodfellow* [1986]; *A-G's Reference* (no. 3 of 1994)

- Series of controversial decisions have held D might be held guilty even if V self-injected

- Kennedy [1999] — D prepared and gave syringe of heroin to V, who injected and died; CA HELD D liable as secondary party [criticism: how can there be secondary party without a principal offender?]

- *Dias* (2001) — similar facts to *Kennedy*; CA agreed analysis in *Kennedy* was flawed, but might be situations where supplied is guilty of manslaughter as principal

- *Rogers* (2003), CA — D held tourniquet while V injected self, died. HELD: D had actively participated; gave extremely wide meaning to 'administered'

- *Finlay* (2003), CA — Question for jury whether D caused the substance to be administered; not necessary to prove actions were sole and immediate charge

– *Kennedy (no. 2)*(2005), HL — Finlay; Rogers wrongly decided; rejected appeal - this was not a case of 'combined operation.' When a person freely and deliberately injects themselves; the supplier cannot be held liable for the act or the consequences.

### 7.5.3. Manslaughter by Gross Negligence

– Modern approach requires high degree of proof for negligence

- *Andrews v DPP* [1937] 2 ALL ER 552 — reticence to attach felony and capitol results to an inadvertent act.
- *Bateman* (1925) 10 Cr App R 8 — jury instructions: show such disregard for life and safety of other as to amount to a crime against the State
    - But some found this unsatisfactory and shifted way from expressing fault in terms of recklessness: *Stone and Dobinson* [1977] QB 354; *Seymour (Edward John)* [1983] 2 AC 493
    - Regarded as too rigid, HL reverted back to *Bateman* in *Adomako* [1995] 1 AC 171, HL — anesthetist failed to respond to non-breathing patient; died from brain damage. Convicted of MS by GN. HL said three elements to be considered:
        - Duty of Care
            - *Willoughby* [2004] — will usually be a matter for the jury (except in cases of doctor/patient, etc.)
            - *Wacker* [2002] EWCA Crim 1944 — may arise even when D and V were involved in joint unlawful enterprise
            - *Lewin v CPS* [2002] EWHC 1049 — D left drunk friend in car on hot day; friend died — no DC, could not be foreseen friend would die
            - *Ruffell* [2003] 2 Cr App R (s) 53 — D deliberately left friend, who had been unwell, in cold; HELD: was a breach of DC
            - *Evans* [2009] EWCA Crim 650; Daughter and mother (Ds) of D's half-sister; who injected herself with OD of heroin; showed signs of overdose; decided against calling for help because all three were addicts and worried about getting in trouble; HELD: liable because didn't take reasonable steps
        - Must be breach of duty amounting to gross negligence

- *Attorney General's Reference* (No. 2 of 1999) — no need to prove D foresaw risk of death
- *Adomako* has been criticized on apparent circularity; law uncertain; jury required to decide issue of law; R V G )2004) liability should not be based on objective fault
- These issues addressed in *Misra* [2004] EWCA Crim 2375 — Hospital doctors; post-op care; patient wound became infected; toxic shock syndrome; died. Following *Adomako*, trial jig ordered jury to convict MS by GN if they were sure conduct fell so far below standard expected of such doctors; Doctors appeal under ECHR Art 7
- WHAT HAPPENED?
- Breach caused death

### 7.5.4. Reckless Manslaughter

- *Hyam* — anyone who kills having foreseen D or GBH has high probability as guilty of murder
- *Moloney* [1985] — foresight, in absence of intention to kill or cause GBH; would no long suffice for murder. But will for MS.
- This basis of liability rarely relied upon because usually D is also guilty of constructive MS and/or MS by GN. This only relevant where D charged with Murder

## 7.6. Proposed Reforms

### 7.6.1. Manslaughter ranges too much: killer who takes conscious and deliberate risk of causing death; person who neither intended nor foresaw.

### 7.6.2. See quote of Lord Lace CJ in *Walker* (1992) 13 Cr App R (S) 474, 476:

*It is a truism to say that of all the crimes in the calendar, the crime of manslaughter faces the sentencing judge with the greatest problem, because manslaughter ranges in its gravity from the borders of murder right down to those of accidental death. It is never easy to strike exactly the right point at which to pitch the sentence.*

# TABLE OF AUTHORITIES

## CASES

*Adomako* [1995]
*Airdale NHS Trust v Bland* [1993]
*Andrews v DPP* [1937]
*Attorney General's Reference (No. 2 of 1999)*
*Attorney General's Reference (No. 3 of 1994)* [1993]
*Bateman* (1925)
*Cato* [1967]
*Church* [1966]
*Cunningham* [1982]
*Dalby* (1982)
*Dias* (2001)
*DPP v Newbury* [1977]
*Evans* [2009]
*Finlay* (2003)
*Franklin* [1883]
*Goodfellow* [1986]
*Hyam* [1975]
*Kennedy (no. 2)* (2005)
*Kennedy* [1999]
*Lamb* [1967]
*Lewin v CPS* [2002]
*Lowe* [1973]
*Matthews and Alleyne* [2003]
*Misra* [2004]
*Mitchell* [1983]
*Moloney* [1985]
*Powell and Daniels; English* [1999]
R *v Malcherek;* R *v Steel* [1981]
*Re A (conjoined twins)* [2000]
*Rogers* (2003)
*Ruffell* [2003]
*Seymour (Edward John)* [1983]

*Stone and Dobinson* [1977]
*Vickers* [1957]
*Wacker* [2002]
*Walker* (1992)
*Willoughby* [2004]
*Woollin* [1999]

**STATUTES**
British Nationality Act 1948 s.3
Coroner's and Justice Act 2009 s.54, 56
Coroners and Justice Act 2009 s.52
ECHR Art 7
Homicide Act 1957 s.2
Homicide Act 1957 s.4
Infant Life (Preservation) Act 1929 s.1
Law Reform (Year and A Day Rule) Act 1996, s.1
Offenses Against the Person Act 1861
Offenses Against the Person Act 1861 s.23
Theft Act 1968 s.9(1)(a)

**TERMS**
in rerum natura

# 8. Voluntary Manslaughter – Defences of Loss of Control and Diminished Responsibility

## 8.1. Loss of control

### 8.1.1. Introduction

- This partial defense replaces the common law partial defense of provocation, abolished by Coroners and Justice Act 2009 s.56; new defense found in s.54(1) - reduce murder charge to manslaughter
- Ingredients:

### 8.1.2. Loss of self-control

- not necessary that D *completely* lose control — *Richens* (1994) 98 Cr App R 43
- Need not be sudden
  - Classic formulation in *Duffy* [1949]: 'under a sudden and temporary loss of self-control, rendering him so subject to passion as to make him for the moment not master of his mind'
  - Not denied because delayed reaction, but must be attributable to the provocation (but longer the interval, less likely it will be successful) — *Ahluwalia* [1992] 4 All ER 889
  - Questions about gender differences here
  - strange that s.54(2) says it need not be sudden—but isn't a loss of self-control always sudden?; also strange that it says it cannot be out of revenge

### 8.1.3. Must be result of a 'qualifying trigger — s.54(1)(b)

– *Fear of serious violence*

- (not a complete defense like self-defense)
- Available where D overreacted and he force was excessive
- D genuinely feared serious violence, does not have to be reasonable fear; against himself or other person (but not in general)

– *Justifiable sense of being seriously wronged* (anger trigger)

- limited to extremely grave things (presumably objective)

– *Combined triggers* (the two above)

– Limitations — s.55(6)(a)-(c)

- D's fear of violence, or sense of being seriously wrongs, to be disregarded if D incited to provide excuse for violence
- sexual infidelity no excuse

### 8.1.4. The Evaluative Question

– Objective: person of D's sex, age, with normal degree of tolerance and self-restraint, might have reacted same way

– short temper, etc., may not be taken into account; history of abuse can be

– if a mental disorder affected actions, reduced liability from murder to manslaughter possible

## 8.2. Diminished Responsibility

### 8.2.1. Statutory defense applying only to murder; available to both principles and secondaries (but not attempted murder) — *Campbell* [1997]

### 8.2.2. Burden of Proof

– If D pleads, balance of probabilities — s.2(2); *Dunbar* [1958] 1 QB 1

- If D raises defense of insanity, prosecution can raise diminished responsibility BRD; Criminal Procedure Insanity Act s.6; *Grant* [1960] Crim L R 424
- Plea can be accepted by judge where medical evidence is not disputed — Cox (1968) 52 Cr App R 130

### 8.2.3. Elements of the defense

- Abnormality of mental functioning which arose from recognized medical condition
    - Recognized psychoses (e.g., schizophrenia); mood disorders (depression); neuroses (phobias, PTS Syndrome); conditions (dementia, epilepsy), but also PMS, battered woman syndrome, morbid jealousy
    - Medical Evidence
        - availability of defense is for jury to decide, not medical experts
        - If nothing in acts or circumstances case doubt on it, bound to accept it — *Dix* [1981]; *Walker* [2009] EWCA Crim 1829).
        - *Byrne* [1960]; *Matheson* [1958]; *Kiszko* [1978]; *Sanders* [1991] Crim LR 781; *Salmon* [2005] EWCA Crim 70;
    - Substantial impairment of specific abilities in respect to
        - ability to under stand nature of conduct (similar to *M'Naughten* Rules)
        - ability to form a rational judgment
        - ability to exercise self-control
- Abnormality provides explanation for D's acts/omissions in killing
    - must cause or be significant factor in causing D's act/omission —need not be sole cause
- Relationship with insanity

- Insanity limited to diseases of the mind affecting perception, understanding, cognition — 'all or nothing'

– DR only requires substantial impairment: a matter of judgment and degree

### 8.2.4. Alcohol, Drugs, and Diminished Responsibility

– Transient effects of drugs/alcohol

- *Di Duca* (1959) 43 Cr App R 167 — transient effects do not constitute an abnormality of mind, cannot diminish responsibility

– Mental Abnormality and intoxication

- The fact that D was intoxicated does not *prevent* a successful pleas of DR if otherwise it would be successful
- . *Hill* (2008) — under old law, HELD: D's abnormality would not have resulted in significant impairment if not for the alcohol, defense was NOT available. Would probably be the same under new rule

– Alcohol Dependency Syndrome

- recognized medical condition — *Tandy* (1989)
- *Stewart* [2009] EWCA Crim 593 — depends on the jury's findings to the nature and extent of the

ADS (under old law, but probably same under new)

## TABLE OF AUTHORITIES

**CASES**
*Ahluwalia* [1992]
*Byrne* [1960]
*Campbell* [1997]
*Dix* [1981]
*Duffy* [1949]
*Dunbar* [1958]
*Grant* [1960]

*Hill* (2008)
*Kiszko* [1978]
*Matheson* [1958]
*Richens* (1994)
*Salmon* [2005]
*Sanders* [1991]
*Stewart* [2009]
*Tandy* (1989)
*Walker* [2009]

**STATUTES**

Coroners and Justice Act 2009 s.54(1)
Coroners and Justice Act 2009 s.54(1)(b)
Coroners and Justice Act 2009 s.55(6)(a)-(c)
Coroners and Justice Act 2009 s.56
Criminal Procedure Insanity Act s.6

# 9. Simple Non-Fatal Offences Against the Person

## 9.1. Common Assault

### 9.1.1. covers both assault and battery

### 9.1.2. 'common' = no aggravating circumstances

### 9.1.3. Offenses Against the Person Act s.47 did not define, just provided maximum penalties

- Assault occasioning actual bodily harm: 5 years
- s20 ( more serious than A&B) Malicious wounding or inflicting GBH: 5 years
- s18: (even more serious) Wounding or causing GBH with intent: Life 9.1.4. Criminal Justice Act 1988 s.39 — did not define, just stated they are summary offenses, penaltie
  - Assault: £5,000 or 6mo or both
  - Battery: £5,000 or 6mo or both

### 9.1.5. No proof of harm needed

- if so, may be aggravated forms might be added

### 9.1.6. A&B are 'gateway offenses' and not serious on their own : aggravated forms are much more serious

- constructive manslaughter can result from A and/or battery

## 9.2. Assault

### 9.2.1. Actus Reus

- where the D cases another to apprehended the application of immediate unlawful force with intent or recklessly

– Concerned with what V apprehends, not D's intention

– Need not be hostile, rude, or aggressive; V need not be afraid, only apprehend it

– Immediacy: need not be instantaneous

- *Smith v Chief Superintendent of Woking Police Station* (1983) 76 Cr App R 234 — was assault to stand outside V's window stare in, her in a short pink nightdress, with intention to scare her

- *R v Horseferry Road Metropolitan Stipendary Magistrate ex parte Siadatan* (1991) 1 QB 260 (QBD) — 'proximity in time and proximity in causation,' 'relatively short time and without any other intervening occurrence'

- *Constanza* [1997] Crim LR 576 — D sent lettres, drove past door often, made silent phone calls; V feared he had 'flipped' and something could happen at any time; CA ruled judge was right to leave Q to jury; 'fear of violence at some time not excluding the immediate future'

– Omissions

– Words may negate what otherwise might be assault

- *Turberville v Savage* (1669) 1 Mod Rep 3 — argument; 'if it were not assize time I would not take such language from you' — no assault

- *R v Meade* (1823) 1 Lew CC 184 — no words or singing could be assault

- *R v Wilson* [1995] 1 WLR 493 — 'get out the knives' could be assault

- *R v Ireland and R v Burstow* [1998] AC 147; (1997) 4 All ER 225, HL — words alone, and sometimes silence, could be assault.

### 9.2.2. Mens Rea

– Intention or recklessness (intended to cause, or was aware of a risk of causing — *Venna* [1976] QB 421

- Recklessness is subjective: prove BRD that D foresaw the risk of of causing V to apprehend — *Savage and Parmenter* [1991] 4 All ER 698

## 9.3. Battery

### 9.3.1. infliction of immediate unlawful violence (no harm or injury needed)

- *Callis v Gunn* [1964] 1 QB 495 — wrongly taking a person's fingerprints: battery
- *Pursell v Horn* (1838) 7 LJ QB 228 — throwing water at V (but not at clothes being worn)
- *Collins v Wilcock* [1984] 3 All ER 374 — Police tapping person on shoulder—not; but subsequent restraint could be
- Ordinary touching in the course of daily life is not
  - *Wilson v Pringle* [1986] 2 All ER 440 — touching much be hostile
  - *Re F* [1990] 2 AC 1 — doubted the term 'hostile' meant anything more than daily acceptable touching
- No battery by omission
  - Fagan v MPC [1969] 1 QB 439 — *drove car onto policeman's foot; refused to move it: court ruled it was a continuing action, guilty of battery. (strains the word 'act'?)*
  - . *DPP v Santana-Bermudez* [2003] All ER (D) (Nov) — drug addict, searched by policewoman; falsely told her no needles, she was pricked by syringe in D's pocket; QB court ruled guilty of s47 OAPA which requires proof of assault or battery
- Direct
  - Need not be direct — throwing a stone suffices; using an implement to trip a V
  - *Martin* [1881] 8 QBD 54 — turned off lights in a thaeter and barred the exits causing a crush

- *DPP v K* [1997] — schoolboy put acid into hot air drier [overruled, but not on this point]
- *Haystead v Chief Constable of Derbyshire* [2000] 3 All ER 890 — D punched A who was holding a baby, child fell hitting head. D was guilty of battery in respect to the child

### 9.3.2. Mens Rea

– Intention/recklessness to inflict unlawful violence on a person (*Venna* [1976])

## 9.4. Consent as a Defense to Assault and Battery

### 9.4.1. Limits on consent

– Crown Prosecution *Service v Shabbir* [2009] EWHC 2754 — spurious point as to whether a lack of consent was a necessary ingredient of the offense or whether it was a defence

– Consent must be specific, but can be implied: holding arm out to Dr for an injection; being jostled in a crowd (*Wilson v Pringle; Re F*)

### 9.4.2. Consent Must Be Real

– Fraud: R *v Williams* [1923] 1 KB 340 — D falsely represented that sex was a breathing exercise to improve singing; D guilty of rape/battery

– Fraud: must go to very nature of the act

- *Clarence* (1888) 22 QBD 23 — D has sex with his wife knowing he had a STD, did not tell her; no deception as to nature of act
- However, R *v Tabassum* [2000] — examined breasts of women who believed it was a medical purpose; consent in relation to nature, but not quality (new element)

– *Feston Konzani* [2005] EWCA Crim 706— conviction of inflicting GBH for having unprotected sex HIV positive without telling women; consent to unprotected sex is not the same thing as consent to risk contracting an infection

– *Dica* (2004) — ruled an adult can consent to risk of STD

– Fraud: Identity of the Person (may vitiate consent)

– Duress — may vitiate consent, may be implied from the relationship — *Nichol* (1807) [schoolteacher and schoolboy, tried to argue consent]

– Capacity — is not vitiated by age if victim understands the nature of the act — *Gillick v West Norfolk Health Authority* [1986] AC 112 — person under 16 could consent to advice and treatment without parental consent

  - But some acts will never be vitiated by consent: Sexual Offenses Act 2003; Tattooing of Minors Act 1969: see *Burrell v Harmer* [1967]

  - Person of full age may lack capacity — T v T [1988]; *Re F* [1989]

### 9.4.3. Public Policy

– Even true consent may be vitiated on these grounds — *Attorney-General's Reference (No. 6 of 1980)* [1981] 2 All ER 1057 — two men, fistfight: HELD: infliction of BH more than transient or trifling and where such was intended but not caused, consent will only be a defense where the harm caused or intended was in the public interest

– *Donovan* [1934] — D caned a 17-year-old girl for own sexual gratification; victim's consent was immaterial

– Sado-Masochism

  - *1) Brown* [1993] — approved *Attorney-General's Reference (No. 6 of 1980)* — Ds were a group of sadomasochistic homosexuals; acts of violence against each other, private gathering; no one complained; came to attention of police while investigating another matter; convicted under OAPA; HL HELD: prosecution does not have to prove lack of consent on part of B before they establish A's guilty, concern for corruption of young men; spread of AIDS (but since this case, *Dica* [2004] ruled an adult can consent to risk of STD), things could get out of hand; D's complained to

ECHR under Art 8 ECHR; *Laskey v United Kingdom* (1997) 24 EHRR 611 — rights under Art 8 are not absolute, of interference in private life was necessary for democratic society in pursing protection of health and morals

- Medical Treatment — therapeutic medical treatment, surgery, with consent, it lawful (also gender change and cosmetic surgery; and live organ donation under strict rules)
- Bodily adornment/mutilation
  - within certain limits _ parent can consent to child's ear-piercing; but courts unwilling to accept some foreign cultural practices, i.e., incision of cheeks' (*Adesanya* (1974) *The Times* 16 July)
- Sports
  - vitiated if assault/battery occur which can reasonably be expected within a game — *Barnes* [2005] EWCA Crim 3246
- Lawful Correction or Chastisement —moderate and reasonable force ok (not spite, anger, gratification)

### 9.4.4. Other Defenses may be allowed (self-defense, necessity — see Ch 12)

## TABLE OF AUTHORITIES

**CASES**

*Adesanya* (1974)
*Attorney-General's Reference (No. 6 of 1980)* [1981]
*Barnes* [2005]
*Brown* [1993]
*Burrell v Harmer* [1967]
*Callis v Gunn* [1964]
*Clarence* (1888)
*Collins v Wilcock* [1984]
*Constanza* [1997]
*Dica* (2004)
*Donovan* [1934]

*DPP v K* [1997]
*DPP v Santana-Bermudez* [2003]
*Fagan v MPC* [1969]
*Feston Konzani* [2005]
*Gillick v West Norfolk Health Authority* [1986]
*Haystead v Chief Constable of Derbyshire* [2000]
*Laskey v United Kingdom* (1997)
*Martin* [1881]
*Nichol* (1807)
*Pursell v Horn* (1838)
R *v Horseferry Road Metropolitan Stipendary Magistrate ex parte Siadatan* (1991)
R *v Ireland and* R *v Burstow* [1998]
R *v Meade* (1823)
R *v Tabassum* [2000]
R *v Williams* [1923]
R *v Wilson* [1995]
*Re F* [1990]
*Savage and Parmenter* [1991]
*Service v Shabbir* [2009]
*Smith v Chief Superintendent of Woking Police Station* (1983)
*T v T* [1988]
*Turberville v Savage* (1669)
*Venna* [1976]
*Wilson v Pringle* [1986]

**STATUTES**

Criminal Justice Act 1988 s.39
ECHR Art 8
Offenses Against the Person Act s.18
Offenses Against the Person Act s.20
Offenses Against the Person Act s.47
Sexual Offenses Act 2003
Tattooing of Minors Act 1969

# 10. Assault Occasioning Actual Bodily Harm

## 10.1. Assault occasioning actual Bodily Harm (Offences Against the Person Act 1861 s47)

### 10.1.1. Must prove that D committed an assault or battery and that the A or B caused ABH

– Smith and Hogan: s.47 does not appear to create another offense; but *Courtie* [1984] says it does

– Consider first whether there was an A or B; then whether harm suffered was ABH; then, did A or B cause ABH

### 10.1.2. Actus Reus

– Actual Bodily Harm definition: any physical injury committing either Assault or Battery

- *Chan Frook* [1994] 2 All Er 552 — includes psychiatric injury, approved by HL in *Ireland and Burstow*
- *Miller* [1954] 2 QB 282 — 'any bodily harm more than transient or trifling'
- *DPP v Smith* [2006] EWHC 94 (Admire) — cutting hair without consent
- *T v DPP* [2003] Crim LR 622

– Occasioning

- must prove that the conduct cause ABH — *Roberts* [1971]

### 10.1.3. Mens Rea

1. same as common assault or battery (ABH is additional actus reus ut not corresponding mens rea); confirmed by Savage; Parmenter (1991)
2. Prosecution does not need to show that defends intended to cause ABH or was reckless as to whether reckless, only that D did.

## 10.2. Malicious Wounding or Inflicting GBH (Offences Against the Person Act 1861 s20)

### 10.2.1. Actus Reus: wounding or Inflicting GBH

– GBH (diff from Bodily harm in degree)

- *Saunders* [1985] Crim LR 230 — 'serious bodily harm'

– Wound (not a scratch)

- *Moriarty v Brooks* (1834) 6 C&P 684 — breaking continuity of skin

– *Burstow (1997)* — no necessary to be force applied to body, psychiatrist abuse enough

- *JCC v Eisenhower* [1983] 3 All ER 230
- *DPP v Smith* [1961] AC 290
- *Janjua and Choudhury* [1999] 1 Cr App R 91
- *Clarence* [1888]
- *Wilsom* (1984)

### 10.2.2. Mens Rea

– S.20 describes as maliciously: requiring proof that the D was aware conduct carried risk of some harm, albeit not serious — *Savage and Parmenter* approving *Mowatt* [1967] 3 All ER 47

- enough that he should have foreseen that some physical harm to some person, even if minor, might result

## 10.3. Racial or Religious Aggravation (Crime and Disorder Act 1988 s29)

10.3.1. If at time of committing or immediately before or after, D demonstrates hostility towards V based on V's membership (presumed or real) of a racial or religious group

10.3.2. Courts have taken a wide view of what constitutes a race or racial group — *DPP v M* [2004] EWHC Crim 1453

10.3.3. *R v Rogers* [2007] UKHL 8 — Spanish women walking along road, 'bloody foreigners,' 'go back to your own country' was enough; though D argued that if they'd said 'bloody Spaniards' would be in violation, but HL saw construction as flexible, non-technical; answered certified questions in the affirmative

## 10.4. Wounding or Causing GBH with Intent and Malicious Wounding with Intent to Resist or Prevent Arrest (Offences Against the Person Act 1861 s18)

10.4.1. Two offenses

- Malicious wounding with intent
  - MW with intent to do GBH
  - MW with intent to resist arrest
  - MW with intent to prevent arrest
- Causing GBH with intent
  - Causing GBH with intent to do GBH
  - Causing GBH with intent to resist arrest
  - Causing GBH with intent to prevent arrest

10.4.2. Does not matter if D did not achieve objective of GBH or resisting/preventing arrest, only that D intended to

10.4.3. Actus Reus

- Same as above: wounding and GBH

- *Mandair* [1995] 1 AC 208, [1994] 2 All ER 715 — judge is entitled to leave to a jury conviction under s20 as an alternative to s18 because term 'causing' is wide enough to include 'inflicting'

### 10.4.4. Mens Rea

- Offenses are often charged in the alternative (D can be charges with ss18, 20, 47 of OAPA 1861; and if jury is not satisfied BRD of one, might be of another
- *R v Hadson (Danielle)* [2009] EWCA Crim 1590 —argued that judge should have left alternatives of unlawful wounding; CA held that no automatic requirement to do so
    - Maliciously give its proper meaning (*Cunningham*-type recklessness)
- *Morrison* [1989] Cr App R 17 — police entered house, D tried to get out through window, police grabbed, injured as D jumped out — CA held maliciously bears subjective meaning, jury should have been directed to consider whether D foresaw risk
- *R v Gregory (Matthew)* [2009] EWCA Crim 1374 — trial judge did not instruct jury according to specimen directions outlined by Judicial Studies Board and in according with *R v Purcell* [1986] 83 Cr.App.R 45; CA held that specimens did not need to be followed slavishly

### 10.4.5. Important: in order to convict under s18, V does not need to actually suffer GBH, only that there was intention to cause harm

## 10.5. Prosecuting policy

### 10.5.1. CPS offers guidelines, not legally binding

### 10.5.2. consistency

### 10.5.3. Policy matter consideration that it is not always appropriate to bring most serious charge possible

- Legal definition of ABH, more tan transient, but if minor black eye, charge s39 not s47

### 10.5.4. Question of ABH and GBH is question for jury

# TABLE OF AUTHORITIES

**CASES**

*Burstow* (1997)
*Chan Frook* [1994]
*Clarence* [1888]
*DPP v M* [2004]
*DPP v Smith* [1961]
*DPP v Smith* [2006]
*Janjua and Choudhury* [1999]
*JCC v Eisenhower* [1983]
*Mandair* [1995]
*Miller* [1954]
*Moriarty v Brooks* (1834)
*Morrison* [1989]
*Mowatt* [1967]
R *v Gregory (Matthew)* [2009]
R *v Hadson (Danielle)* [2009]
R *v Purcell* [1986]
R *v Rogers* [2007]
*Roberts* [1971]
*Saunders* [1985]
*Savage; Parmenter* (1991)
*T v DPP* [2003]
*Wilsom* (1984)

**STATUTES**

Crime and Disorder Act 1988 s29
Offences Against the Person Act 1861 s18
Offences Against the Person Act 1861 s20
Offences Against the Person Act 1861 s47

# 11. Sexual Offences

## 11.1. The Social context of sexual offences

### 11.1.1. What is rape?

– usually not violent, D usually knows V, male or female

– inaccurate view of rape in general

### 11.1.2. Level of sexual offending

– lack of reporting, evidential problems in assessing consent

– underreported and under-recorded

## 11.2. Law Reform Process

### 11.2.1. history

– Sexual Offences Act 1956, amended in 1994 and 2000 (brought male rape and marital rape into definition)

– 2000 — began process of reforming law on sexual offences: *Setting the Boundaries* consultation paper

– 2002 – White Paper, *Protecting the Public*

– Bill drafted, became Sexual Offenses Act 2003

### 11.2.2. Needs

– date rape, date rape drugs, etc. modernization ideas and practices

– Human Rights Act 1998 compatible (due process v victim rights and public protection)

# 11.3. Rape (SOA 2003 s.1)

## 11.3.1. Actus Reus

– max penalty of life

– SOA 2003 widened AR more than previous legislation:

- Penetrations of vagina, anus, mouth
  - no presumption that one more serious than another — *Ismail* [2005] EWCA Crim 2936
  - penetration is a continuing act, same as common law in *Kaitamaki* [1985] AC 147
- with penis (therefore, can only be committed by a man)
- V does not consent

– 'unlawful' removed, marital rape now included — *R v R* [1992] 1 AC 599

## 11.3.2. Mens Rea

– Intentional penetration

– lack of reasonable belief that V consented

- belief must be both honestly held and reasonable (objective)
- not necessary that V say "I consent;" jury may take into account age, mental capacity, previous relationship

# 11.4. Assault by Penetration (SOA 2003 s.2)

## 11.4.1. New offense created by SOA 2003 s.2 (deliberate overlap with other offense)

## 11.4.2. Actus Reus

– Penetrates vagina or anus

– with part of body or anything else —can be committed by either man or woman, victim of either gender

– V does not consent

– Penetration is sexual

- to distinguish liability between sexual offenses and non-sexual assaults
- definition (s.78) confirms common law meaning of 'indecent' as in *Court* [1989] AC 28

– of its nature is sexual (if a reasonable person would think so)

– of nature may be sexual, *and* the circumstances or purpose or both is sexual (deals with ambiguous acts)

– purpose, not motive (as in all criminal offenses)

### 11.4.3. Mens Rea

– intentionally penetrates V

– Lacks reasonable belief in V's consent

## 11.5. Consent

### 11.5.1. Must be shown that V did not consent, and D did not reasonably believe that V consented

### 11.5.2. If V does not consent, or consent is invalid for reasons in ss.75, 76, then *prima facie* liability, now D's state of mind is to be examined regarding V's consent

### 11.5.3. For problem questions, approach in reverse order of relevant statute sections:

– s.76 — **Conclusive Presumptions**: Consent invalid if D intentionally deceived as to nature and purpose of act; OR impersonated someone personally know to V no need to move on to s.75 or s.76

- deceit as to nature of act: SOA s.76(2)(a) same as in *Flattery* (1877) 2 QBD 410 — D told V he was performing surgery, but actually having sexual intercourse — no causal link needed
- but SOA goes further, also includes purpose/quality of act: previous courts had been going with quality of act

(aware act is sexual, but deceived as to why); now purpose is enough — no causal link needed

- Identity — confirms common law position in *Elbekkay* [1995] Crim LR 163, attempt to impersonate a husband/partner; SOA goes further: anyone personally known — causal link needed— i) Must be causal link between decisions and consent — *Richardson (Diana)* [1998] 2 Cr App R 200 — false qualifications as dentist would not invalidate consent unless they went to nature/ purpose

– s.75 — **Evidential Presumptions** (rebuttable): Consent presumed to be invalid if: violence (actual, threat, or fear of); V was detained and D was not at time; V was asleep/unconscious; physically disabled; caused D to take substance to be stupefied or overpowered at time — no need to move on the s.74

– s.74 — general definition of consent: person consents if he/she agrees by choice, and has freedom and capacity to do so

- very wide definition: time frame is important though
- *R v B* (2006) EWCA 2945 — D did not disclose he was HIV positive to woman in which he had sex; HELD it was not relevant that he failed; it was not relevant to whether she consented to intercourse (if she had contracted the disease, she would have had recourse through s.20 OAP Act

# TABLE OF AUTHORITIES

**CASES**

*Court* [1989]
*Elbekkay* [1995]
*Flattery* (1877)
*Ismail* [2005]
*Kaitamaki* [1985]
*R v B* (2006)

*Richardson (Diana)* [1998]

**STATUTES**

Human Rights Act 1998
Offenses Against the Person Act s.20
Sexual Offences Act 1956
Sexual Offenses Act 2003
Sexual Offenses Act 2003 2.74
Sexual Offenses Act 2003 s.1
Sexual Offenses Act 2003 s.2
Sexual Offenses Act 2003 s.20
Sexual Offenses Act 2003 s.75, 76
Sexual Offenses Act 2003 s.76(2)(a)
Sexual Offenses Act 2003 s.78

# 12. Defenses 1: Failure of Proof and Justificatory Proof

## 12.1. Defenses 1: Excusatory and Mental Disorder Defenses

## 12.2. Failure of Proof

### 12.2.1. Mistake

- Mistakes as to Law
    - ignorance of law no defense
    - exceptions: theft of item because D truly believed it belonged to him — s.2(1) Theft Act 1968 (might be a mistake of fact, though)
    - Mistakes as to fact
    - results in prosecution faiing to prove either AR or MR, if mistake is relevant
    - *Tolson* [1889] — D's husband missing for 5 years, presumed dead, remarried, then discovered he was still alive; her honest and reasonable believe negated AR
        - reasonable and honestly held was disapproved by the HL in *B v DPP* [2002] — need only be honestly held
    - Mistakes as to surrounding circumstances
        - 1) *William (Gladstone)* [1984] Crim LR 163 — general rule, needs to be honestly held but not necessarily reasonable [D saw boy called for help being assaulted; V was lawfully arresting youth, but could not provide ID (he was falsely impersonating an officer but performing a lawful arrest) ; D was acquitted

- Drunken mistakes
  - Does not apply when D is intoxicated and the mistake was induced by that intoxication
  - *O'Grady* [1987] Crim LR 706 — D, heavily intoxicated, attached and killed V, believing wrongly V was attacking him with a glass
- Mistakes Relating to Mens Rea
  - *R v G* [2003] — honest but mistaken belief would negate MR; same true in relation to intent (direct or oblique, see *Woollin* [1998]
  - does not apply to sexual offenses under s.104 Sexual Offenses Act 2003; mistaken belief in consent must be reasonably held and honestly held

### 12.2.2. Intoxication

- Limited defense
- Poses a problem in criminal law, because MR may not be there, through fault of D
- *Majewksi* [1977] tried to find legal solution
- Levels of intoxication
  - first determine if D is drunk enough to consider defense (based on a lack of MR)
  - *Sheehan and Moore* [1975] Crim LR 339 : 'a drunken intent is nevertheless an intent'
- Voluntary intoxication
  - If lacks MR, afforded defense
  - Only if crime is specific intent, not basic intent — *Majewski* [1976] 2 All ER 142 — a pub fight; attacked proprietor, , police officer, charged with assault occasioning ABH; claimed large quantity of alcohol and drugs in the 48 hours before; HL adopted approach outlined in *DPP v Beard*

[1920] AC 479 of defining crim offenses into the two categories

    - Basic and Specific Intent Crimes

  - Basic Intent: can be committed recklessly, voluntary intoxication NO defense (prior fault in getting drunk, provides MR for act committed)
  - Specific Intent: only intent will suffice as MR, voluntary intoxication can be a defense
  - has led to much criticism for lack of legal reasoning and accuracy —breaches principle of contemporaneity, but in some areas actions can be interpreted as ongoing (*Thabo Mell* [1954]; *Fagan* [1969]), but *Cunningham* [1957] recklessness says that it must involve a foresight of risk.
  - *Heard* (2007)

– Involuntary Intoxication

  - Not possible to apply *Majewski*, lacks MR, makes no difference if basic or specific intent
  - But if offense does not require MR (strict liability) then it is no defense

3) *Kingston* [1994] 3 All ER 353

#### 12.2.3. Soporific Drugs — but makes D unusually aggressive, make not be reckless under *Majewski* — *Hardie* [1985] 3 All ER 848; D took valium, set fire to GF's flat; unpredictability allowed defense;*Bailey* (1983)

## 12.3. Justificatory Defences

### 12.3.1. Justifications

– Substantive defenses: due to special circumstances, D may be partially or wholly not to blame

– Two kinds: Excusatory (see ch 13) and Justificatory — not wrong in law or principle

  - Chose lesser of two evils

- Responding to a morally wrong conduct by V, who forfeits right to protection

– in order to uphold rights under law

– Public officers in pursuit if duty

### 12.3.2. Self-Defense

– Four Sources

- s.3 Criminal Law Act 1967 — permits reasonable force in the prevention of crime or making lawful arrest of someone committing a crime
- *Owino* [1996] 2 Cr App R 128 — two stage test: D (1) believes honestly that force is necessary to defend self, another, property and (2) used reasonable force — confirmed in *R v Palmer* [1971] 1 All ER 1077
- s.176 Criminal Justice and Immigration Act 2008 — complex law attempting to clarify requirements of 'reasonable force'
- s.5 Criminal Damage Act 1971 — similar to common law defense, only applies to offense of criminal damage: lawful excuse if D honestly believed it was necessary to protect property

– Force used must be necessary

- judged from D's perspective (subjective) — *William (Gladstone)* [1984] — only if mistake induced by intoxication that it must be reasonable, see *O'Grady* [1987] (do not confused with level of force)
- Criticized on human rights grounds, Art 2 ECHR
- Reasonable to use force rather than peaceably escape — *Bird* [1985] 1 WLR 816
- Pre-emptive strike is okay if reasonable — *Beckford* [1988] AC 130
- If D provokes force or trheat, cannot be used as self-defense — *Brown* [1972]

    - If unintentional provocation, may still be able to rely on self-defense — *Balogun* [1999]
    - May use force to protect property if reasonable — *Martin* (often misunderstood: convicted of murder of burglar of his house; CA ruled killing was not reasonable, not that he couldn't defend his home

- Force Used Must Be Reasonable
    - *Owino* [1995] — established
    - May be a question of proportionality in some cases, how much force to protect a work of art or a house or to prevent rape; always judge by jury taking into account all circumstances
- Defense cannot be used to reduce a charge, all or nothing (might be able to plead loss of control to reduce though)

### 12.3.3. Necessity

- often said to be 'lesser of two evils'
- courts traditionally reluctant to allow
- *London Borough of Southwark v Williams* [1971] 2 All ER 175; civil wrong of trespassers to avoid homelessness, prosecuting such would open a door to no one being safe in home
- *Dudley and Stevens* [1884] — four men marooned at sea, killed and ate cabin boy; convicted of murder not allowed necessity defense; ratio of this case was addressed in *Re A (conjoined twins)* 2 WLR 480
- It is no general defense except in exceptional circumstances
- See *Re F (mental patient: sterilization)* [1990] 2 AC 1 — patient unable to consent; HL held it was in patients best interest; lawful, defense of necessity applies
- So, Defense of necessity may be available at common law where
    - in best interest of patient

- D has statutory duty to act (police officer, see *Johnson v Phillips* [1975]
- In exceptional cases such as *Re A* where it is necessary and proportionate to avoid an inevitable evil

# TABLE OF AUTHORITIES

**CASES**
*B v DPP* [2002]
*Bailey* (1983)
*Balogun* [1999]
*Beckford* [1988]
*Bird* [1985]
*Brown* [1972]
*Cunningham* [1957]
*DPP v Beard* [1920]
*Dudley and Stevens* [1884]
*Fagan* [1969]
*Hardie* [1985]
*Heard* (2007)
*Johnson v Phillips* [1975]
*Kingston* [1994]
*London Borough of Southwark v Williams* [1971]
*Majewksi* [1977]
*O'Grady* [1987]
*Owino* [1995]
R *v* G [2003]
*Re A (conjoined twins)* [2000]
*Re* F *(mental patient: sterilization)* [1990]
*Sheehan and Moore* [1975]
*Thabo Mell* [1954]
*Tolson* [1889]
*William (Gladstone)* [1984]
*Woollin* [1998]

**STATUTES**
Criminal Damage Act 1971 2.5
Criminal Justice and Immigration Act 2008 2.176

Criminal Law Act 1967 s.3
Sexual Offenses Act 2003 2.104
Theft Act 1968 s.2(1)

**TERMS**
Basic Intent
prior fault
Specific Intent

# 13. Defenses 2: Excusatory and Mental Disorder Defenses

## 13.1. Excusatory Defences

### 13.1.1. Duress

- Pressure put upon D which compels him to act unlawfully
- Must involve serious threat of death or serious injury
  - 'will was overborne'
- not physically forced, but morally forced
- Not a defense to murder (*Howe* [1987]) or attempted murder (*Gotts* [1992])
- Courts expect highest degree of heroism, and self-sacrifice — see *Howe*
- Duress is a complete defense — *DPP v Lynch* (1975)

### 13.1.2. Threats

- Threats to D or another
  - Can be threats against other people — *Pommell* [1995] 2 Cr App R 607; *Conway* [1988; *Martin* [1989]
  - Threat cannot come from D himself — *Rodger and Rose* [1998] 1 Cr App R 143
- Threat must Be Operative
  - D must believe threat will be carried out if he does not commit crime
  - It must be the threat which compels D to act, not some other reason — *Valderrama-Vega* [1985] Crim LR 220

– D must Not Put Himself in a Position Where he Is Likely to Be Threatened

- example: join a gang — *Sharp* [1987]; *Shepherd* [1988]; drug addict-dealer — *Heath* [2000] Crim LR 109

– Mistake as the Threats

- okay, provided mistake is reasonable — *Graham* [1982], honest believe not enough (inconsistent with mistakes as to surrounding circumstances are dealt with in relation to other offenses such as self-defense and provocation — criticized in *Safi* [2003] Crim LR 721)

– Threat of Imminent Harm

- No avenue of escape — *Hudson and Taylor* [1971] 2 All ER 244; *Heath* [2000]; *Hasan* [2005] UKHL 22: could have sought police protection
- imminent enough to be operating on the mind of D at the time of the crime

– Reasonable Response to Threat

- 'sober person of reasonable firmness' sharing D's characteristics — *Graham* [1982]
- *Bowen* [1996] 1 Cr App R 157 addressed characteristics
  - level of firmness (age, sex, mental illness/psychiatric condition
  - capacity to escape (age, physical ability)
  - which affect gravity of threat (pregnancy)
  - not self-induced (alcohol, drug addiction)

### 13.1.3. Circumstances

– This defense created almost accidentally by the courts in *Willer* (1986) 83 Cr App 225

– developed in series of road cases: *Conway* [1988]; *Harris* [1994]

- *Pommell* [1995] — confirmed that the defence did exist and could apply to all except murder and attempted murder
- Is there a general defense of necessity? differences suggest no
    - Defense of duress of circumstances not available for murder/attempted i) But *Re A* suggests the defense of necessity is available to charge of murder
    - Duress of Circumstances requires imminent threat;
        - necessity does not (just some unavoidable evil)
    - Duress of circumstances may excuse D's conduct i) Defense of Necessity justifies the conduct
    - duress of circumstances may be defense where no threat exists but D mistakenly and reasonably believes it does
    - Necessity will fail unless there is an actual 'unavoidable evil'

## 13.2. Mental Disorder Defences

### 13.2.1. Insanity

- Can apply to any defense
- basically a denial of MR
- term is outdates, no long applied in medical field, it is a legal term
- Claim: D must first be judged 'fit to plead' (fit to stand trial) — *Antoine* [2001]
    - if so, can proceed and plead insanity or automatism
    - No mental control over actions, an automatron
- Most prefer automatism which results in acquittal
- insanity used to be compulsory committal
    - since 1991, court can determine to detain, place under supervision, or discharge

### 13.2.2. Components of the Defense of Insanity

- Procedure
  - Prosecution must prove AR, no need to prove MR
  - D then proves lack of MR by showing that he fulfills test of insanity set out by *M'Naghten* [1843]
  - disease of the mind
    - not a medical question, but a legal one — *Sullivan* [1984] 1 AC 1512
    - impairment of reason, memories, understanding — Bratty [1963]
    - causes of disease do not matter
    - does not matter if it is permanent or transient
- Distinction between internal factors (insanity) and external factors (automatism)
- defect of reason
  - the disease of mind must cause a defect of reason
  - *Clarke* [1972] 1 All ER 219 — depression did not count, just a momentary lapse in concentration
- D did not know the nature and quality of his act
  - must result in either a lack of knowledge of the physical nature of act, or the quality of the act
- D did not know what he was doing was wrong
  - *Windle* [1952] 2 QB 826 — husband killed wife by overdose our of mercy; had been caring for her for some time; depressed and claimed he suffered from folie à deux (person caring for mentally ill person becomes mentally ill); defense failed because he knew actions were wrong, even though he believed they were not morally wrong
- If irresistible impulse leads D to not be able to appreciate the wrongness of actions, defense maysucceed — *Sodeman* [1936]

### 13.2.3. Sane Automatism

- Outcome is acquittal
- Only succeeds where lack of control is from external cause and there is NO control over actions — *Attorney General's Reference (No. 2 of 1992)* [1994] QB 91 — lorry driver, 6 hours riving, without awareness, crashed and killed two people; was partially in control though

### 13.2.4. Automatism and Intoxication

- Voluntary consumption of non-prescription drugs
- Courts have applied rules from *Majewski*
    - specific intent: D may be acquitted
    - basic intent: will depend on what caused the intoxication

### 13.2.5. Reform

- antiquated definition of 'disease of mind'
- Law Commission Draft Criminal Code 1989 proposed alternatives using terms severe mental illness or severe mental handicap as alternatives
    - lasting impairment memory, orientation, comprehensions, learning capacity
    - alteration of mood to such a degree to give rise to delusional appraisals
        - delusional beliefs, persecutory, jealous, grandiose
        - disordered thinking to prevent reasonable appraisal of situations or communication

# TABLE OF AUTHORITIES

**CASES**

*Antoine* [2001]
*Attorney General's Reference (No. 2 of 1992)* [1994]
*Bowen* [1996]

*Clarke* [1972]
*Conway* [1988]
*DPP v Lynch* (1975)
*Gotts* [1992]
*Graham* [1982]
*Harris* [1994]
*Hasan* [2005]
*Heath* [2000]
*Howe* [1987]
*Hudson and Taylor* [1971]
*M'Naghten* [1843]
*Martin* [1989]
*Pommell* [1995]
*Rodger and Rose* [1998]
*Safi* [2003]
*Sharp* [1987]
*Shepherd* [1988]
*Sodeman* [1936]
*Sullivan* [1984]
*Valderrama-Vega* [1985]
*Willer* (1986)
*Windle* [1952]

# 14. Attempt

## 14.1. Attempt

### 14.1.1. Actus Reus

– doing of an act which is more than preparatory for the commission of a substantive offense

– must take steps

– Role of judge and jury

- whether act is more than preparatory is for jury
- judge decides whether act could amount to an attempt

– Complete and incomplete attempts

- does all he/she believes necessary, but fails
- steps, but not taken final step
- Gullefer **[1990] 3 All ER 882** — bet on greyhound; looking like losing; jumped onto track to distract; hope to have race declare void; recover money; Did not interfere with race; charged with attempted theft; HELD: no; jump onto track; then go to bookmaker and demand money; did not get beyond preparation stage
- Jones **(1990) 91 Cr App R 351** — D got into car driven by ex-mistress new lover; pointed a loaded, sawn-off shotgun; V grabbed hold, threw out window; safety catch was still on; finger not on trigger: HELD: convicted of attepted murder; had obtained, shortened, loaded; disguised; got in car, took out gun; pointe at victim
- . *Attorney-General's Reference (No. 1 of 1992)* [1992] 96 Cr App R 298; Crim L R 274 — attempted rape, not necessary that D attempts physical penetration; anything jury considers more than merely preparatory

– Two 'troubling cases'

- Campbell **[1991] 93 Cr App R 9199** — D loitering around post office; wearing crash helmut; sunglasses; carrying heavy object; looked around and left; came back 30m later was arrested; possession of imitation gun and threatening note; admitted he intended to commit robbery; HELD: all those acts merely preparatory

- Geddes **[1996] Crim LR 894** — D trespassing in lavatory block of Brighton school; large knife and rope and masking tape; evidence he intended to kidnap a child; HELD: conduct did not go beyond mere preparation; lying in weight is not enough for an attempt; should ask 'did he try' to commit the offense, or only put himself in position to do so

### 14.1.2. Mens Rea of Attempt

– Meaning of intent

- D must intend the act or conduct element of the substantive offense

- D must intend the consequences of the substantive offense

  - *O'Toole* [1987] Crim LR 759 — though reckless as to causing damage will suffice for arson, attempted arson must include evidence that D intended to cause damage

– Conditional intent

- *Husseyn* (1977) Cr App R 131D — opened door of van holding sub-aqua equipment; charged with attempted theft; trial judged directed jury D could be convicted if he looked inside with intention of stealing contents if they were valuable; HELD: misdirection; cannot be said that one who has in mind to steal if valuables has a present intention to steal

- *Attorney-General's Reference (Nos 1 and 2 of 1979)* [1980] QB 180 — overcame problem of *Husseyn* with procedural solution: can be convicted of attempted theft even if he finds nothing worth stealing provided the indictment states he intended to steal 'some or all of the contents'

– D must know existence of circumstances element of substantive offense, or, if a lesser form of fault required for an ofense, must know there is a risk the circumstances exist

- Khan **[1990]** — charged with attempted rape; at that time substantive offense required proof man ad sex with woman who did not consent and he knew it or was reckless as to whether she consented; HELD: means rea is same in rape as in attempted rape: intention to have sex + knowledge of or recklessness as to consent

- Attorney General's reference **(No. 3 of 1992)** — D threw petrol bombs at car with passengers, miss car; charged with attempted aggravated arson being reckless as to endangerment of life; trial judge directed jury that D had to b proved that he intended the lives of others to be endangered, recklessness not enough: HELD: recklessness would suffice

- Law Commission (Law Com No 318 (2009)) rejected this approach: if D need be subjectively reckless as to substantive offenses, same for attempt; where lesser form required for substantive offense; subjective recklessness still okay for attempt; with higher form of fault required for substantive offense, same fault element for attempt

### 14.1.3. Attempting the Imossible

– Criminal Attempts Act 1981 s.1(2) person may be guilty even if facts are such that commission is impossible

– Shivpuri **[1987]** HL — D found in possession of bags of powder; thought he was importing heroin; was vegetable material; convicted; HELD: an impossible attempt is still an attempt

– Taafe **[1984]** — D enlisted to take packages to UK; D thought it was money; thought it was illegal; it was actually cannabis; HELD: not guilty of any offense; he did not intent to import pot and there is no offense of importing currency

- Offenses which cannot be attempted
  - only offenses triable on indictment — cannot be guilt of attempting a summary offense (i.e., assault or battery)
  - attempting to conspire
  - attempting to aid, abet, counsel, or procure an offense (but can be guilty of attempting to incite)
  - attempt by omission
- Successful attempts
  - can be convicted of attempt even if he successfully commits the full offense

# TABLE OF AUTHORITIES

**CASES**

*Attorney General's reference (No. 3 of 1992)* [1993]
*Attorney-General's Reference (No. 1 of 1992)* [1992]
*Attorney-General's Reference (Nos 1 and 2 of 1979)* [1980]
*Campbell* [1991]
*Geddes* [1996]
*Gullefer* [1990]
*Husseyn* (1977)
*Jones* (1990)
*Khan* [1990]
*O'Toole* [1987]
*Shivpuri* [1987]
*Taafe* [1984]

**STATUTES**

Criminal Attempts Act 1981 s.1(2)

**OTHER**

Law Com No 318 (2009)

# 15. Parties to Crime

## 15.1. The framework of Secondary Liability

### 15.1.1. Accessories and Abettors Act 1861 — does not create offense of 'being a secondary party' (aid, abet, counsel, procure)

### 15.1.2. Terminology — *Bryce* [2004] EWCA Crim 1231 — accomplices, accessories, secondary parties (latter is preferable)

### 15.1.3. Modes of participation

- *Attorney General's Reference (No. 1 of 1975)* [1975] 2 All ER 684 — words should be given ordinary meaning
- Howe [1987] AC 147 — former technical discinctions between categories now redundant; three modes:
  - encouraging
  - assisting
  - procuring
- Commission of the Principal Offense — Secondary liability is derivative, only attaches when offense

committed

## 15.2. Actus Reus

### 15.2.1. Aid

- any type of assistance prior to or at time of
- does not have to be sine qua non
- principle need not be aware

### 15.2.2. Abet or counsel

– encouraging, must have come to attention of principal

– need not be sine qua non — *Calhaem* [1985] 2 ALL ER 266 — D2 paid D1 to murder V; went to houses, but no intention of doing it, just wanted to scare; V screamed, D1 went berserk and hit her, killing her; D2 convicted of murder as secondary, appealed; HELD: dismissed, actual offense committed, contact and counseling between the counseling and the murder

### 15.2.3. Procuring

– *Attorney General's Reference (No. 1 of 1975)* — to produce by endeavor, set out to see something happens then take appropriate steps to produce it — secretly laced D1's drink with alcohol; D1 drove home DUI; D2 procured the offense

– No requirement they have communicated with each other, esp. important in cases of strict liability

– Apply to crimes requiring mens rea where D2 caused D1 to commit actus reus but not guilty as principle because of lack of mens rea, incapacity, or availability of defense

- *Cogan and Leak* [1975] — could be convicted as accomplice to rape though perp was acquitted due to lack of mens rea
- *DPP v K and B* [1997] — D can be convicted of rape as a procurer, despite prosecution unable to rebut presumption (req'd at time) that alleged perp (under 14) lacked capacity
- *Bourne* [1952] — offense committed by secondary party though principal was excused on grounds of duress

## 15.3. Mens Rea

### 15.3.1. Intro

– several elements

– *Rook* [1993] 2 All ER 955, accepted in *Bryce* [2004] mens rea requirements are the same in all cases of secondary liability

### 15.3.2. The Act of Assistance, encouragement or procuring was done intentionally and D2 knew it to be an act capable of assisting, encouraging or procuring the offense

– Accidental assistance will not attract secondary liability

- *Clarkson* [1971] — Accused was present when woman raped in barracks; some actively assisted; no evidence Cdid any acts or any encouragement; convicted of aiding and abetting but conviction was quashed; must be intention to encourage mere presence, even deliberate, is not enough
- *Bryce* — must intend to assistant or encourage; intention to hinder with negate 15.3.3. At the time of the act of assistance/encouragement/procuring D2 foresaw the commission of the offense by D1

– A general principle

- Foresight is the basis, not necessary that the party intended the crime to be committed — *NCB v Gamble* (1959) 42 Cr App R 240
- *Lynch v DPP for Northern Ireland* [1975] AC 653 — D2 drove D1 to a garage where he knew D1 intended to murder a policeman; intentional driving of car not enough; not necessary that D2 knows that a crime will be committed; sufficient that he foresaw it as a real or substantial risk or a real possibility
- *Bainbridge* [1960] 1 QB 129 — Supplied D1 with oxygen cutting equipment; used to break into bank; should not have been convicted unless he knew that's what it would be used for i) Reformulated by HL in DPP for Northern Ireland v Maxwell [1978] 3 ELL ER 1140; maxwell part of a terrorist organization in NI; ordered to drive car to inn; knew others were armed, make some attack but didn't know with what; they planted a bomb; rightly convicted; some knowledge that violence would be resorted to
- *Hyde and Others* (1991) 92 Cr App R 131 — three attacked V, died from kick to head; not possible to know who did it; judge directed that if all three intended to do GBH, all

shared in liability; CA dismissed; if D2 realizes that D1 may kill or inflict GBH, and participates, sufficient mens rea to be guilty

- Approved by HL in *Powell and Daniels* [1999] AC 1 — P&D went with X to drug dealer to buy drugs, shot drug dealer; unable to prove who fired; guilty of murder because they knew he had gun; appeals dismissed: sufficient for secondary liability if he knew might kill with intent or kill with intent to GBH; must foresee
- *Rook* [1993] 2 All ER 955 — also where secondary party lends assistance encouragement or assistance before crime
- *Reardon* [1999] Crim LR 392 — D1 shot two men in a pub; along with others, D2 carried Vs out; D1 stays with the dying men; went back into pub, told D2 one of them men alive asked for knife; D2 gave him; D1 went out killed both; D2 convicted of murder; CA dismissed: were within the scope of contemplation when he handed knife

– The level of foresight required

- Need not see precise events — *Miah (Aziz)* [2009] EWCA Crim 2368

– Foresight of an act of the type committed by D1

- Must foresee an act of the type which is committed — Hyde — character of weapon too different; others not liable
- *English* [1997] 4 All ER 545 — D1/D2 attack with wooden posts; D1 produced knife and stabbed V to death; HL HELD: knife was fundamentally different from wooden post
- *Greatrex* [1999] 1 Cr App R 126 — group of youth attacked V, died from blow from bar/spanner; CA HELD: judge should have directed jury to consider whether G foresaw possibility of whether of use by bar or other dangerous weapon — 'fundamentally different act' rule

- View accepted by HL *Rahman* [2008] UKHL 45 — rejected idea that jury should be allowed to take the intent of D1 into account when deciding whether is fact was fundamentally different from that of D2

– Whether the act was fundamentally different is a question of fact for the jury

- *O'Flaherty* —
- *Mendez* [2010] EWCA Crim 516

– D2 is not a party to killing if the Acts f D1 are fundamentally different from those foreseen

- no liability if actions are of a different type than contemplated by others; may still be guilty of offenses they did commit — *Uddin* [1998]
- *Anderson and Morris* [1966] 2 All ER 644 — killed with a knife; D2 defense was took part in attack, but through to beat up, no idea there was a knife; trial judge help jury could convict D2 of manslaughter even if he had no idea; CA held it was misdirection, quashed conviction

– Where D1 performs an act foreseen by D2 but with a more serious intent

- *Gilmour* [2000] Cr App R 407 — D2 drove three men to house, knowing a petrol bomb would be throw nat property; 3 children died from fire; D2 thought it was only to frighten; CA HELD: guilty of manslaughter
- *Roberts, Day and Day* [2001] EWCA Crim 1594 — participants all foresaw kind of physical violence but different in intent; 2 intended very serious injury; other saw some harm; D1 punched kicked; suffered brain hemorrhage and died; D1 and D2 held guilty of murder; D3 joint enterprise to inflict some harm; not negated by larger intentions of other two
- *Attorney General's reference (No. 3 of 2004)* [2005] EWCA Crim 1882 — D2 sent men to apply pressure to V, knew

they were armed with gun, might fire to frighten; not foreseen they might kill or injure; one fatally shot V in head; HELD: D2 not guilty; was of a fundamentally different character to any act contemplated by D2 (Distinguished *Roberts, Day and Day* basis that that act was not fundamentally different)

- Liability for unforeseen consequences
  - *Anderson; Morris* [1966] — Where D2 is liable for acts of D1, that liability extends to unusual or unforeseen consequences
  - The Secondary Party May be Liable for More Serious Offense than the Perpetrator
  - If D1 suffers from abnormality of mind, and D2 assists or encourages D1 to kill or GBH, D1 reduced to manslaughter, D2 guilty of murder — Homicide Act 1957 s.2(4)
    - Doctrine of transferred malice applies in secondary liability

## 15.4. Withdrawal

15.4.1. Person can escape secondary liability if they withdraw before act is committed or reached stage of attempt — *Grundy* [1977] Crim L Rev 543

15.4.2. Usually must be an act, just just a mental change; question of fact and degree for jury — *O'Flaherty* [2004] EWCA Crim 526

15.4.3. *Mitchell and King* (1998); *Rafferty* [2007] EWCA Crim 1846 — must be communication of withdrawal to principal unless not practical or reasonable

15.4.4. *Rafferty*; *Campbell* [2009] EWCA Crim 50 — D2 will be liable for acts/consequences carried out before withdrawal

# TABLE OF AUTHORITIES

**CASES**

*Mitchell and King* (1998)
*NCB v Gamble* (1959)
*O'Flaherty* [2004]
*Powell and Daniels* [1999]
*Rafferty* [2007]
*Rahman* [2008]
*Reardon* [1999]
*Roberts, Day and Day* [2001]
*Rook* [1993]
*Uddin* [1998]

**STATUTES**
Accessories and Abettors Act 1861
Homicide Act 1957 s.2(4)

# 16. Theft and Fraud

## 16.1. Theft (Theft Act 1968)

### 16.1.1. Actus Reus

– Appropriation

- most controversial
- assumption of the rights of an owner (innocent or not) and decides to keep/deal as owner
  - *Morris* [1983] 3 All ER 292 — any, if not all, rights: switched labels in supermarket without authority (*obiter*: must be adverse usurpation; conflicted with
  - *Lawrence* [1972] 2 All ER 1253 — Italian student got taxi ride, did not speak English well, offered driver open wallet to take right amount, driver took more: HELD consent was relevant to issue of dishonesty, not relevant to determining whether appropriation had take place
  - *Gomez* [1993] AC 442 — ass't mngr of a shop, friend asked to supply goods in exchange for stolen cheques, D told boss checks had been ok'd by bank; owner did consent; HELD: not right to interpret Act as saying that authorization/consent could never amount to misappropriation; confirmed *Lawrence*, *Morris* was *obiter dicta.*
  - Widened further in *Hinks* [2000] 4 All ER 833 — D befriended V, elderly man of limited intelligence; V withdrew sums of money while with D and gave them to D; HELD: after *Gomez*, consent was irrelevant; made 'appropriation' virtually meaningless as consent is ok and manner is meaningless

- Property
    - money, all other property real or personal, things in action (debt; credit balance; cheque) and other tangibles
        - land is tangible but not property for the purposes of the offense of theft; exceptions: rights over land; tangible parts of land (topsoil); taking of fixtures
    - *Oxford v Moss* (1978) 68 Cr App R 183 — student took exam paper, read it, returned it: HELD: not guilty of theft of info
    - flowers, fruit, etc. cannot be stolen by picking unless for commercial purposes or sale
    - wild animals: only if kept in captivity (poaching is a different offense); carcass only if taken into possession
- Belonging to another
    - having possession, control, proprietary right or interest
    - May belong to more than one person at a time
    - Can own property without knowing it: *Woodman* [1974] 2 All ER 955 — owner of unused factory, sold scrap metal from it, thought all was gone, someone took the leftover; HELD: convicted of theft, they were i possession and controlled even though they did not know it.
    - *Hibbert v McKiernan* (1948) — Golf Club owns golf course, has control over balls lost on it.
    - Can steal something you own: *Turner (No. 2)* [1971] 2 All ER 441 — left car at garage for repair; D secretly took it back with intent to avoid paying; HELD: garage had possession and control at time (and a lien)
        - Contrast *Meredith* [1973] Crim LR 253 — D parked car illegality; police took to station; D went and drove it away: HELD: no theft, police did not have lien could not withhold possession (but could fine him)

### 16.1.2. Mens Rea

– Dishonesty

- Act provides examples of lack of dishonesty: belief (honesty held, not necessarily reasonable). Defenses:
    - that there is a right in law to take (for himself or another)
    - owner would consent
    - owner cannot be discovered by reasonable steps
- Common law additions:
    - *R v Ghosh* [1982] 2 All ER 689 sets out two-part test
    - was it dishonest under ordinary standards of reasonable people? (if no, finished) [objective]
    - did D realize that what he was doing was, by the above standards, dishonest [subjective]
    - See also *Landy* (1981) and *Feely* (1973)

– Intention to permanently deprive

- same meaning as other criminal offenses
- intends to treat thing as own; to dispose of; borrowing/lending may amount, if that is for a period and circumstances that make it the same as taking — *Lloyd* [1985] 2 All ER 661 — film projectionist, borrowing films to copy, returned them in time to show; HELD: did not amount to theft, all the goodness had not gone out (but would be guilty of copyright infringement)
- *Lavender* [1994] Crim LR 297 — took two doors from Council property, used to replace doors at another council property; HELD: treated the doors as his own; 'to dispose of' did not literally mean sell or throw away
- *Fernandes* [1996] Crim LR 753 — 'deals with that property in such a manner that he knows he is risking its loss'

## 16.2. Fraud

### 16.2.1. Law Reform process

- 2002 Law Commission review on deception offences Theft Act 1968 and Theft Act 1978; proposed Draft Bill
    - Theft Act 1968 had obtaining property by deception; pecuniary advantage
- Theft Act 1978 add obtaining services by deception; evading liability by deception
- Theft (Amendment) Act 1996 added obtaining money transfer by deception
- Problems were identifying what had been obtained, whether deception caused it; how offences applied to different scenarios (needed to update for modern situations, technology)

### 16.2.2. Fraud Offenses (Fraud Act 2006)

### 16.2.3. Fraud by False Representation — broad new offense

- as to fact or law or state of mind
    - I am 18 — fact
    - You can sell alcohol to a 17 year old — law
    - enters restaurant with no money and buys food — state of mind
- express or implied (words, omission, behavior)
    - Examples: *DPP v Ray* [1973] 3 All ER 131; *Charles* [1977] AC 177; *Gilmartin* (1983) 76 Cr App R 238; *Lambie* [1982] AC 449
- using a system or device (old Acts: could not deceive machine)
- causation
    - does not actually need to cause a loss; intent suffices
    - V does not have to be deceived (Ormerod claims it criminalizes lying)

– Mens Rea

  - knows it might be false or misleading (covers deliberate and careless deceptions) i) some difficulty in proving that D knew or was aware of risk?

  - intends to make a gain or loss

– No recklessness here: if jury finds foresight as to gain/loss virtually certain, can find intent (*Woollin*)

  - only for money or other property: excludes land; non-pecuniary gains

    - D may gain for self or another

    - acting dishonestly

### 16.2.4. Fraud by Failure to Disclose Information

– Legal Duty to Disclose — from statute, contract of insurance, express/implied terms of contract, trade or market custom, agent/principle relationship, etc.

### 16.2.5. Fraud by Abuse of Position (vague)

– Position to safeguard, or not act against, the financial interests of another

  - trustee/beneficiary, director/company, professional person/client, employee/employer, within family, etc.

– Abuse (need not intend loss by V, but by other party; or for another to make gain)

### 16.2.6. Obtaining Services Dishonestly

– replaces old offense of obtaining services by deception, update to cover electronic and automated services

– free services not covered

– service itself is what is obtained, not monetary value

### 16.2.7. Making Off Without Payment

- Does not require deception, enacted to close loophole in law found in *DPP v Ray* [1973]
- knowing payment is due 'on the spot,' dishonestly makes off without paying with intent to avoid it
- *Brooks and Brooks* (1982) 76 Cr App R 66 — making off need not be by stealth
- No need to identify exact 'spot' — *Aziz* [1993] Crim LR 708 — asked taxi to take him to club 13m away; refused to pay; driver took him to police station; D ran but was caught; claimed he had not left the 'spot'; HELD: spot was where payment was required
- Payment need not be on spot if other arrangements were made — *Vincent* [2001] 2 Cr App R 150 — stayed in hotel; upon leaving agreed to pay later
- Must intend to never pay, not just intend to pay later —*Allen* [1985]

# TABLE OF AUTHORITIES

**CASES**

*Allen* [1985]
*Aziz* [1993]
*Brooks and Brooks* (1982)
*Charles* [1977]
*DPP v Ray* [1973]
*Feely* (1973)
*Fernandes* [1996]
*Gilmartin* (1983)
*Gomez* [1993]
*Hibbert v McKiernan* (1948)
*Hinks* [2000]
*Lambie* [1982]
*Landy* (1981)
*Lavender* [1994]

*Lawrence* [1972]
*Lloyd* [1985]
*Meredith* [1973]
*Morris* [1983]
*Oxford v Moss* (1978)
R *v Ghosh* [1982]
*Turner (No. 2)* [1971]
*Vincent [2001]*
*Woodman* [1974]

**STATUTES**
Fraud Act 2006
Theft (Amendment) Act 1996
Theft Act 1968
Theft Act 1978

# 17. Robbery

## 17.1. Robbery (Theft Act 1968 s.8)

### 17.1.1. Actus Reus

- Stealing
  - all elements of theft must be proved (dishonest appropriation; property; belong to another; intent to permanently deprive
  - *Corcoran v Anderton* (1980) 71 Cr App R 104 — D snatched handbag, ran away, dropped it; HELD: guilty because by time he dropped it the offense was complete
- Force
  - force can be minimal, mere touching suffices — *Dawson and James* (1976) 64 Cr App R 170; *Clouden* [1987] Crim LR 56
  - force must be used in order to steal (causal link)
  - Need not be directed at owner of property
  - Must be used before or at time of stealing, but courts do not interpret strictly
    - *Hale* (1978) 68 Cr App R 415 — two Ds entered V's house, D1 went upstairs to steal, D2 tied V up; force and theft might have been at different times: HELD: theft was a continuing act so they were commensurate
    - *Lockley* (1995)

### 17.1.2. Mens Rea

- Theft Act 1968 is silent to mens rea (but mens rea of theft must be met); however, fact that force/threat of force must be used in order to steal implies intent —accidental will not suffice

- Dishonest intent to permanently deprive — *Skivington* (1968); *Robinson* (1977)
- D must intend that V be put in fear (but V need to be in fear)

## 17.2. Burglary (Theft Act 1968 s.9-10)

- *need not involve unlawful acquisition of property*
- *house: max 14 years*
- *commercial = max 10 years*

### 17.2.1. Entering a Building or Part of A Building as a Trespasser

- Enter
  - "Enter" has been a contentious element— whole body? — *Collins* [1972] 2 All ER 1105 — D climbs ladder onto windowsill naked intending to have sex with V; V thinks it is her bf, invited him in; have sx; then V discovers he is not her BF; HELD: he had 'entered' when on windowsill, 'substantial and effective entry' all that was required; jury had not been instructed properly, conviction quashed
  - See *Brown* (1985); *Ryan* (1996)
  - Entry does not have to be forced
- Building
  - Wide definition: caravan, houseboat, barn, garage — *B and S Leathley* [1979] Crim LR 314 — freezer container, locked doors, connected to electricity
  - Must be relatively permanent — *Royal Exchange Theatre Trust v The Commissioners* [1978]
  - Must be complete — *Manning and Rogers* [1871]

  - 'part of a bulding' — can have permission in one part but not another — *Walkington* [1979] 2 All ER 716 — in shop, behind a moveable courter to put his hands in the till

- As a Trespasser
  - trespass is a tort, word bears that meaning here
  - Must not have consent (*Collins* would not have been trespassing if she invited him in before he crossed the threshold)
  - Stretch point further in *Jones and Smith* [1976] 3 All ER 54 — entered house with father's permission; he and friends stole two telleys; he exceeded permission is that, when he entered, he intended to steal (substantially widened the actus reus)

### 17.2.2. Three ways burglary can be committed

- Section 9(1)(a)
  - intent to commit s.9(2) offenses: theft, GBH, criminal damage — specific intent crime
- Section 9(1)(b)
  - ctually commits theft/attempted theft, infliction/attempted infliction GBH
  - See *Jenkins* (1983)
    - (Trespass with the intent to commit a sexual offense)
  - S.9(1)(a) used to include rape, removed from Theft Act 1968 by Sexual Offenses Act s.63 (as trespasser, intends to commit relevant sexual act, knows or is reckless as to whether he is a trespasser) — offense need not be actually committed
- Aggravated Burglary
  - identical to others, but commits act with
  - firearm (or imitation)

- weapon of offense — *Williams* (1977) — first type is made for causing injury, second is adapted to it (potato with razor blade in it), could be any object
- explosive — See *Francis* (1982); *O'Leary* (1986

## TABLE OF AUTHORITIES

**CASES**

*B and S Leathley* [1979] Crim LR 314
*Clouden* [1987] Crim LR 56
*Collins* [1972] 2 All ER 1105
*Dawson and James* (1976) 64 Cr App R 170
*Francis* (1982)
*Hale* (1978) 68 Cr App R 415
*Jenkins* (1983)
*Jones and Smith* [1976] 3 All ER 54
*Lockley* (1995)
*Manning and Rogers* [1871]
*O'Leary* (1986
*Robinson* (1977)
*Royal Exchange Theatre Trust v The Commissioners* [1978]
*Skivington* (1968)
*Walkington* [1979] 2 All ER 716
*Williams* (1977)

**STATUTES**

Theft Act 1968 s.8
Theft Act 1968 s.9-10
Sexual Offenses Act s.63

# 18. Criminal Damage

## 18.1. Simple Criminal Damage

### 18.1.1. Actus Reus

- Destroy — e.g, demolish a bullding, killing an animal, spraying weedkiller on someone's favorite plant
- Damage — need only be slight (scratching a car, cracking a window)
  - question of fact and degree — *Cox v Riley* [1986]
  - Difficulty is what level is required (what about chalk on sidewalk?) — see *Gayford v Choulder* [1898]; *Hardman v Chief Constable of Avon and Somerset Constabulary* [1986]; *A (a juvenile) v* R [1978]; *Morphitis v Salmon* [1990]; *Roper v Knott* [1898]
  - Impairing the usefulness of property can amount to damage — *Woolcock* [1977]
- Property — defined by Criminal Damage Act 1971 s.10(1)
- Belonging to Another

### 18.1.2. Mens Rea (basic intent crime: self-induced intoxication is no defense – *Majewski*)

- Intentional Destruction or damage to property belonging to another
  - must be proved that D intended to destroy or damage
- Reckless Destruction of or damage to property belonging to another
  - Criminal Damage Act 1971 replaced Malicious Damage Act 1861; intended to reflect the definition of 'maliciously' as interpreted by *Cunningham* [1957] 2 QB 396

- CA followed this in *Stephenson* [1979] after the Criminal Damage Act 1971 was enacted
- However, *Caldwell* [1982] AC 341 gave rise to two types: 'advertent' (*Cunningham*) and 'inadvertent' recklessness.
- *Caldwell* subsequently overruled by HL in *R v G* (2003)
- *Castle* [2004] All ER (D) 289 CA held *Caldwell* no longer appropriate, applied *R v G.*
- Recklessness requires proof that D was aware of a risk of damaging property belonging to another and, without justification, too that risk.
- If he genuinely believes the property is his, he is not guilty — *Smith* (1974)

## 18.2. Aggravated Criminal Damage

### 18.2.1. Actus Reus

– same as for simple criminal damage except it is not restricted to 'property of another'

### 18.2.2. Mens Rea

– same as for simple criminal damage

– Must also be proved that D was aware of an obvious and significant risk of danger to life — *Cooper* [2004] EWCA 1382 — D convicted of arson, being reckless as to whether life was endangered; trial judge summed up in accordance with *Caldwell*; CA held that in light of *R v G* [2004], judge must direct jury that danger to life was obvious and significant to the D; if there was a risk but D dismissed it as negligible, cannot say that he realized he was taking an obvious and significant risk.

– Note the link between criminal damage itself and D's ulterior mens rea

## 18.3. Arson

18.3.1. two separate possible counts: arson with intent to endanger life; being reckless as to whether life would be endangered

18.3.2. *Drayton (Alan Clark)* [2005] EWCA — requirement to charge arson also meant requirement to charge as damage by fire, not some other means.

18.3.3. Racially or Religiously Aggravated Criminal Damage — Crime and Disorder Act 1998 s.30(1) (as amended by Anti-Terrorism, Crime and Security Act 2001)

## 18.4. Defenses

### 18.4.1. Lawful Excuse

- BOP remains on prosecution to prove D did not have lawful excuse
- Criminal Damage Act s.5(2) provides a partial definition
- Was D's belief honestly held?
  - Does not need to be a reasonable belief — *R v Jones and others* [2004] EWCA Crim 1981 — charged with a number of offenses including crim damage and arson at RAF base; reason was their beliefs based on lawfulness of actions of the UK in declaring and waging war in Iraq; subject belief ok, only objective element was if the damage could amount to something done to protect another's property; legality of war in Iraq was not relevant
    - If property or interest is in immediate need of protection if threat to property has already materialized — *Chamberlain v Lindon* (1998) *The Times*, 6 April
    - *Hill and Hall* (1989)
    - *Kelleher* (2003) — cut off head of statute of Thatcher in art gallery; argued he did so to bring attention to her policies which made the world more dangerous place, would lead to destruction of Earth; CA HELD:

– May not be available if there is only a tenuous connection with alleged purpose of protecting property — *Hunt* [1977] Cr App R 105

  - Does not matter that the mistake was a drunken mistake — *Jaggard v Dickinson* [1980] 3 All ER 716

  - If there is no evidence of a lawful excuse, judge can withdraw the issue from the jury, but should not be directed to convict — *Wang* [2005] UKHL 9

# TABLE OF AUTHORITIES

**CASES**

*A (a juvenile) v* R [1978]
*Caldwell* [1982]
*Castle* [2004]
*Chamberlain v Lindon* (1998)
*Cooper* [2004]
*Cox v Riley* [1986]
*Drayton (Alan Clark)* [2005]
*Gayford v Choulder* [1898]
*Hardman v Chief Constable of Avon and Somerset Constabulary* [1986]
*Hill and Hall* (1989)
*Hunt* [1977]
*Jaggard v Dickinson* [1980]
*Kelleher* (2003)
*Morphitis v Salmon* [1990]
R *v G* (2003)
R *v Jones and others* [2004]
*Roper v Knott* [1898]
*Smith* (1974)
*Stephenson* [1979]
*Wang* [2005]

**STATUTES**

Anti-Terrorism, Crime and Security Act 2001
Crime and Disorder Act 1998 s.30(1)
Criminal Damage Act 1971

Criminal Damage Act 1971 s.10(1)
Criminal Damage Act s.5(2)
Malicious Damage Act 1861.

# Diagrams

# 1. Introduction

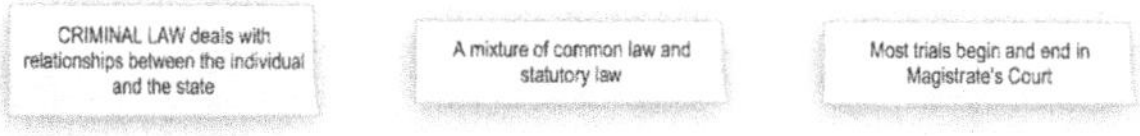


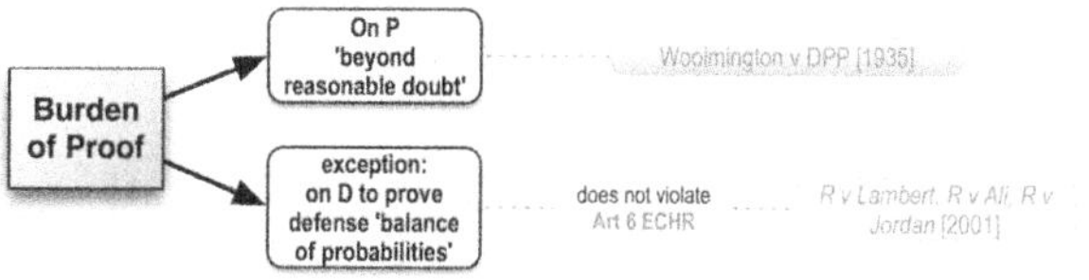

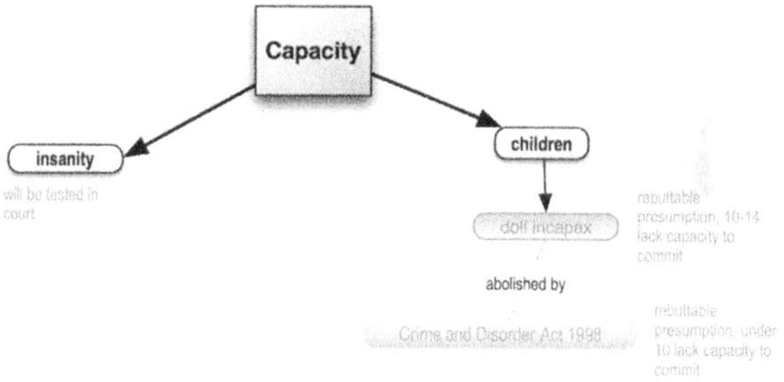

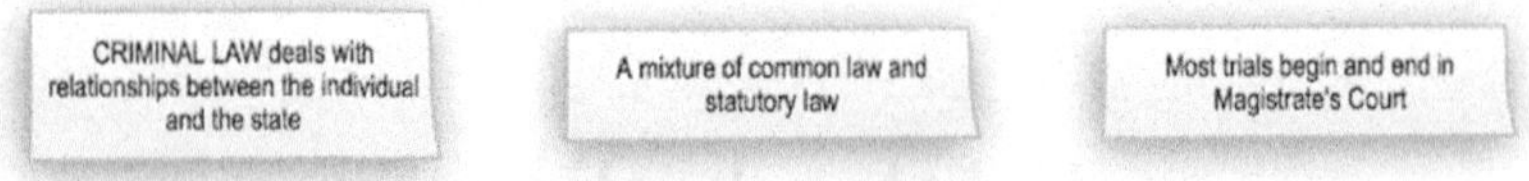
CRIMINAL LAW deals with relationships between the individual and the state
A mixture of common law and statutory law
Most trials begin and end in Magistrate's Court

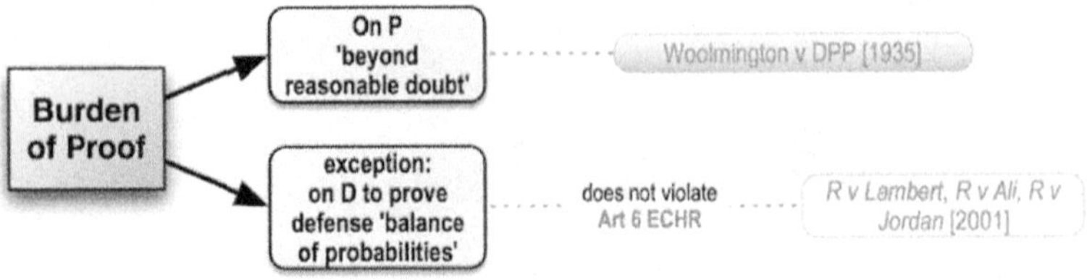
Burden of Proof
On P 'beyond reasonable doubt'
Woolmington v DPP [1935]
exception: on D to prove defense 'balance of probabilities'
does not violate Art 6 ECHR
R v Lambert, R v Ali, R v Jordan [2001]

# 2. Elements of an Offense

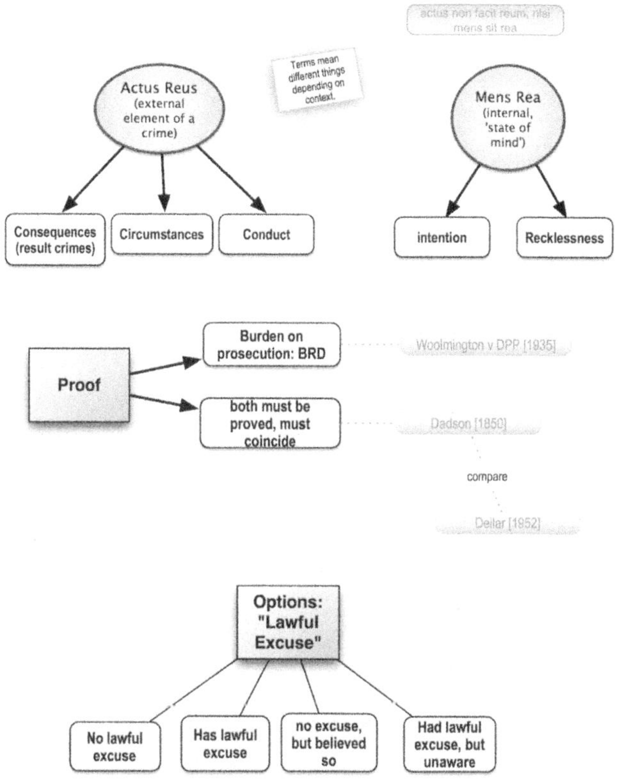

# 3. Actus Reus: Voluntariness

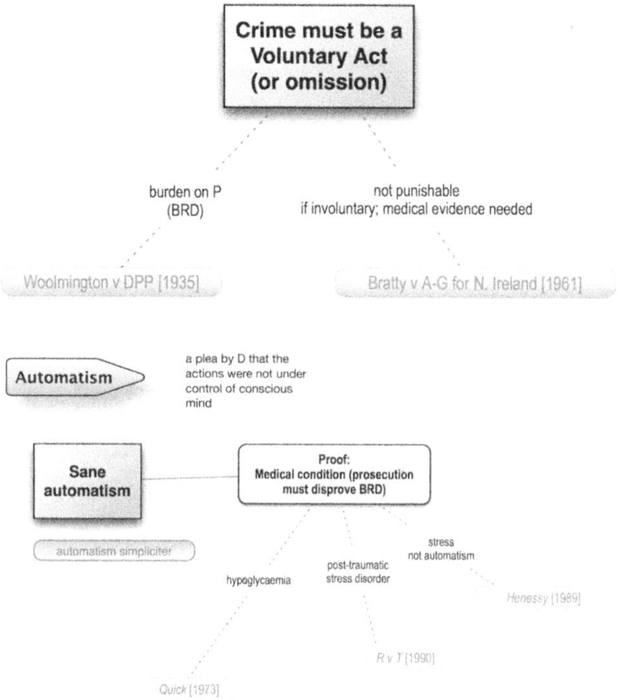

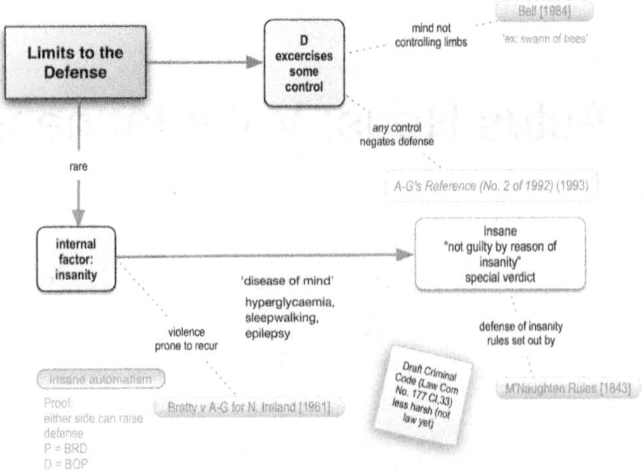
Limits to the Defense
D excercises some control
mind not controlling limbs
Bell [1984]
'ex: swarm of bees'
any control negates defense
A-G's Reference (No. 2 of 1992) (1993)
rare
internal factor: insanity
insane "not guilty by reason of insanity" special verdict
'disease of mind'
hyperglycaemia, sleepwalking, epilepsy
violence prone to recur
defense of insanity rules set out by
Draft Criminal Code (Law Com No. 177 Cl.33) less harsh (not law yet)
M'Naughten Rules [1843]
insane automatism
Proof: either side can raise defense P = BRD D = BOP
Bratty v A-G for N. Ireland [1961]

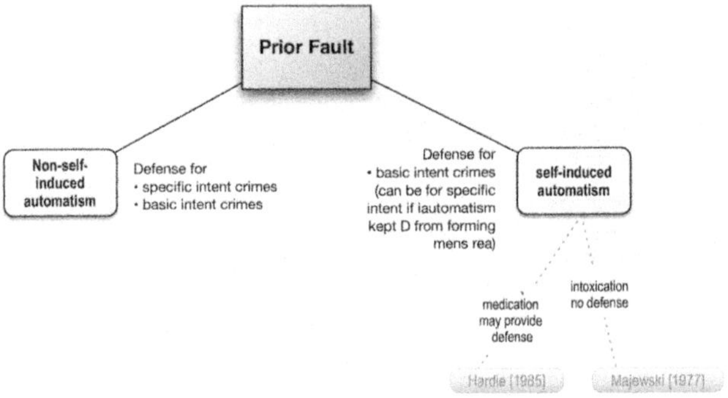
Prior Fault
Non-self-induced automatism
Defense for
• specific intent crimes
• basic intent crimes
Defense for
• basic intent crimes (can be for specific intent if iautomatism kept D from forming mens rea)
self-induced automatism
medication may provide defense
intoxication no defense
Hardie [1985]
Majewski [1977]

# 4. Actus Reus: Omissions

1. Is an offense capable of being committed by omission?
2. Is there a duty of care?

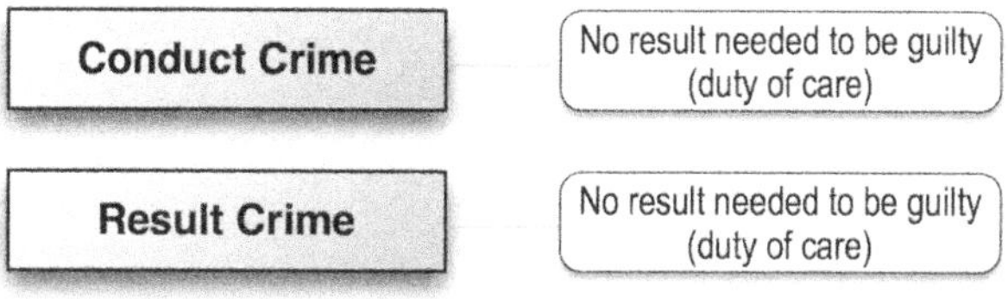


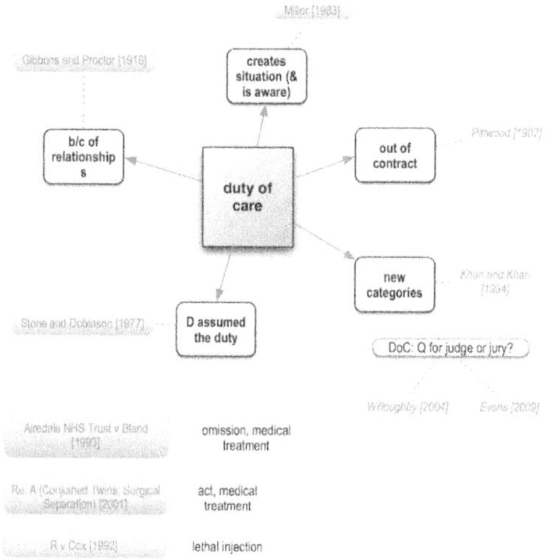

# 5. Actus Reus: Consequences

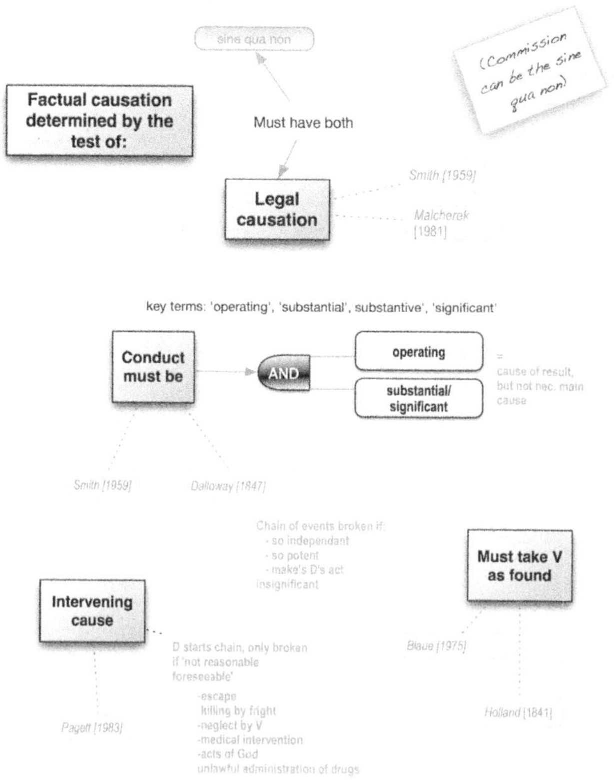

# 6. Mens Rea

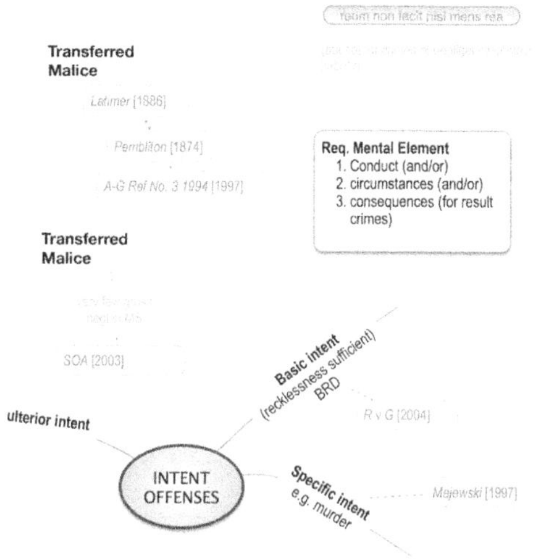

reum non facit nisi mens rea
Transferred Malice
Latimer [1886]
Pembliton [1874]
A-G Ref No. 3 1994 [1997]
Req. Mental Element
1. Conduct (and/or)
2. circumstances (and/or)
3. consequences (for result crimes)
Transferred Malice
SOA [2003]
Basic intent
(recklessness sufficient)
BRD
R v G [2004]
ulterior intent
INTENT OFFENSES
Specific intent
e.g. murder
Majewski [1997]


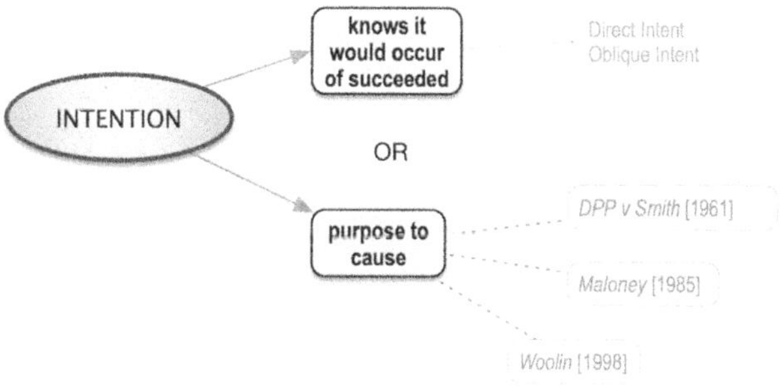

INTENTION
knows it would occur of succeeded
Direct Intent
Oblique Intent
OR
purpose to cause
DPP v Smith [1961]
Maloney [1985]
Woolin [1998]

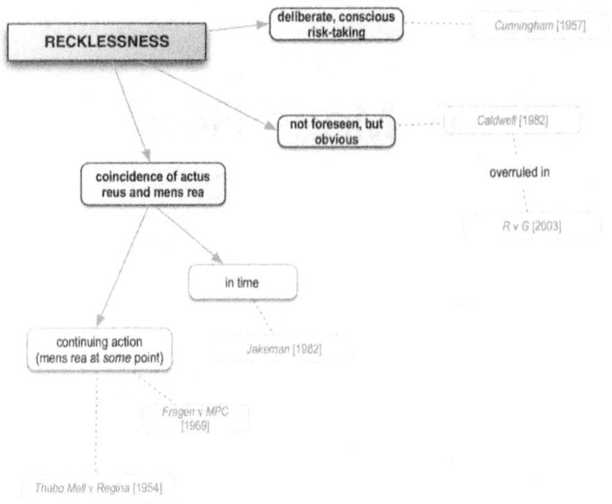
RECKLESSNESS
deliberate, conscious risk-taking
Cunningham [1957]
not foreseen, but obvious
Caldwell [1982]
overruled in
R v G [2003]
coincidence of actus reus and mens rea
in time
Jakeman [1982]
continuing action (mens rea at some point)
Fagan v MPC [1969]
Thabo Meli v Regina [1954]

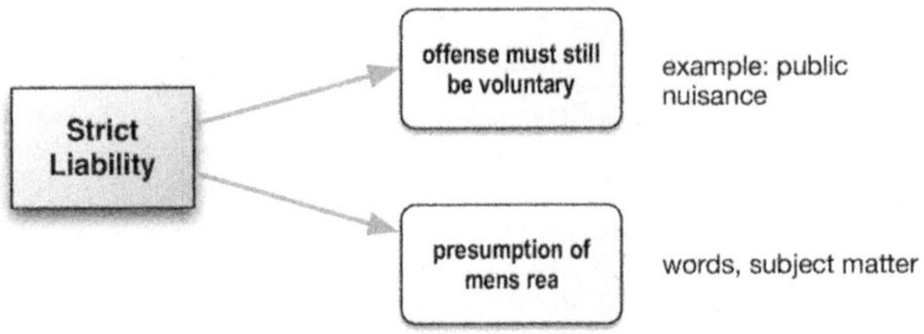
Strict Liability
offense must still be voluntary
example: public nuisance
presumption of mens rea
words, subject matter

# 7. Unlawful Homicide: Murder and Manslaughter

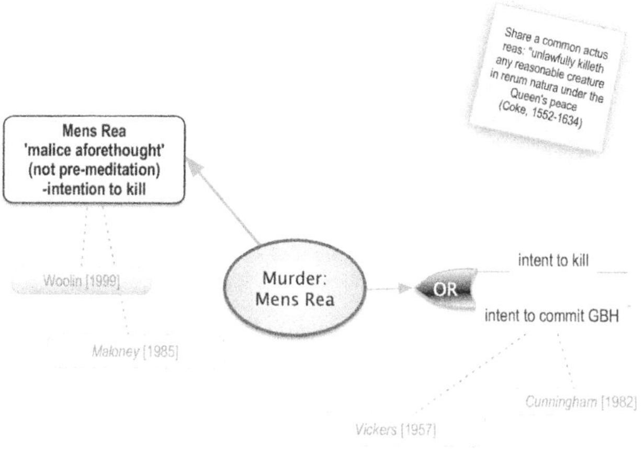


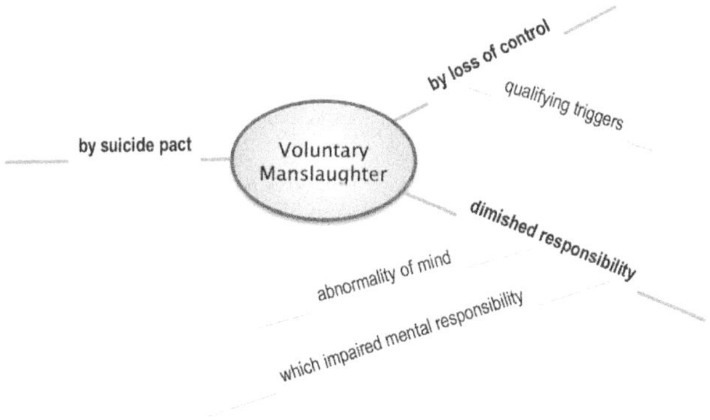

Involuntary Manslaughter
MS by gross negligence
breach of duty owed to deceased
so serious to justify crim liability
In the past = *any* negligence
today = hi degree of negligence
Andrews v DPP [1937]
Bateman [1925]
Constructive MS (MS by unlawful & dangerous act)
objective test: 'reasonable person'
likely to cause some bodily harm
committing an unlawful act
kills another person
unintentionally & unforeseeably
civil wrong insufficient
Franklin [1880]
Andrews [1937]
Reckless MS
deliberately took
an unjustified risk
causing serious injury
not omission
Lowe [1973]

# 8. Voluntary Manslaughter – Defences of Loss of Control and Diminished Responsibility

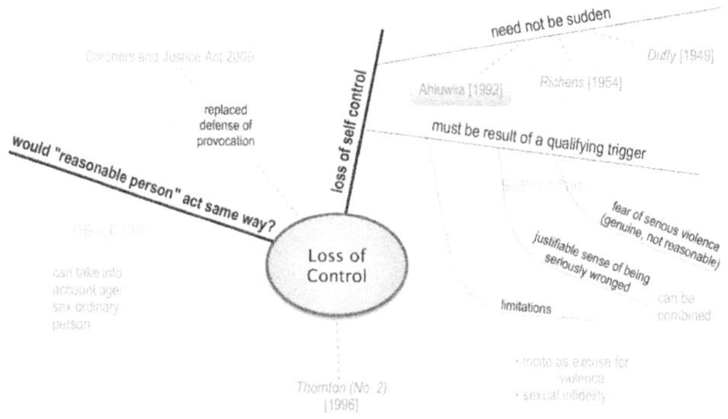


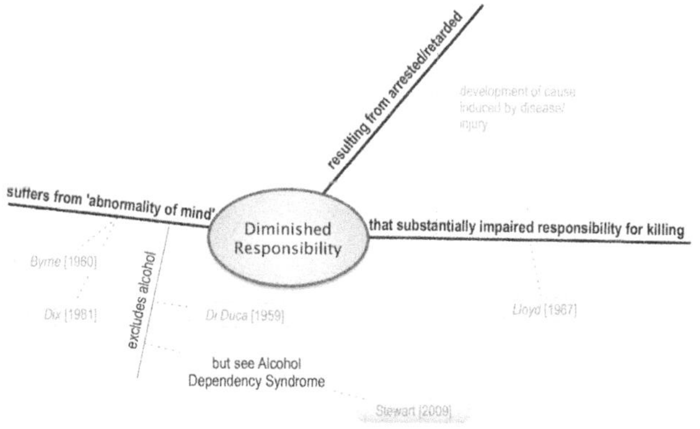

# 9. Simple Non-Fatal Offences Against the Person

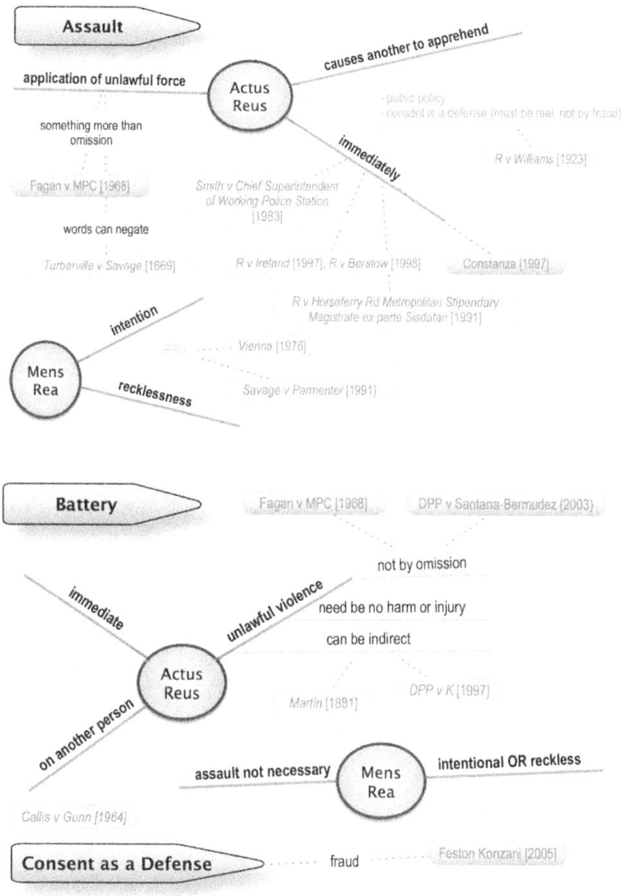

# 10. Assault Occasioning Actual Bodily Harm

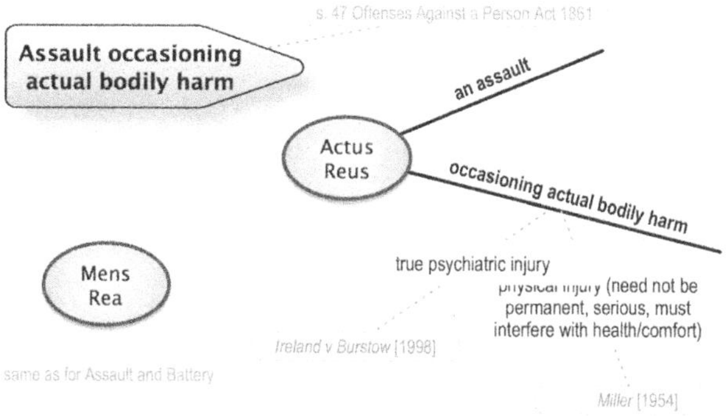


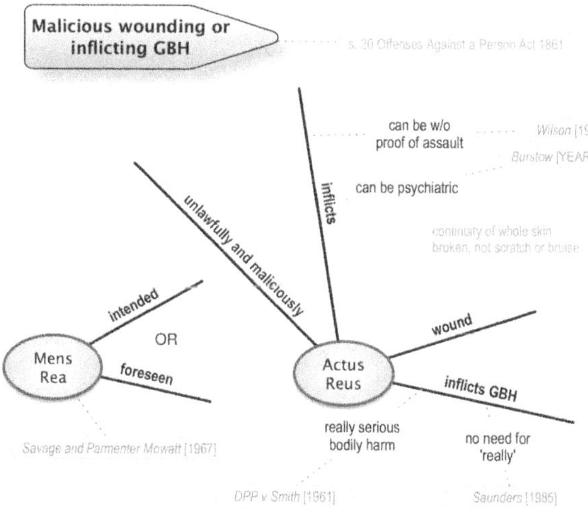

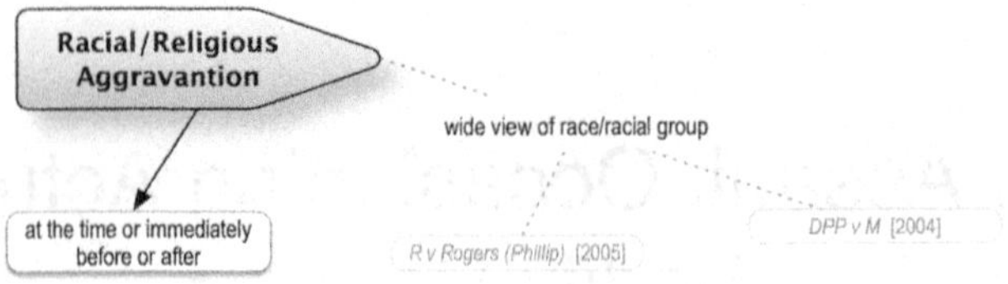
Racial/Religious Aggravantion
wide view of race/racial group
at the time or immediately before or after
R v Rogers (Phillip) [2005]
DPP v M [2004]

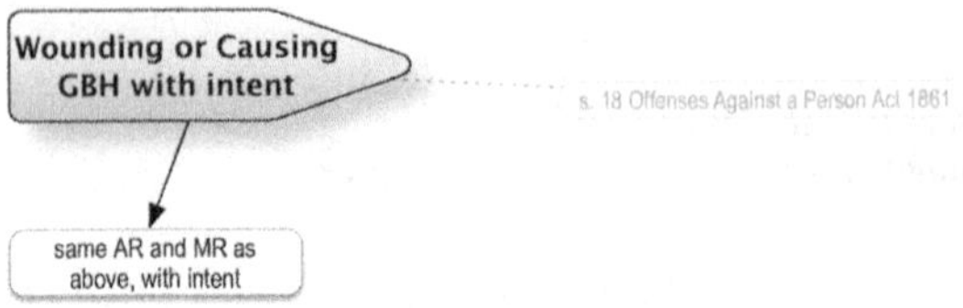
Wounding or Causing GBH with intent
s. 18 Offenses Against a Person Act 1861
same AR and MR as above, with intent

# 11. Sexual Offences

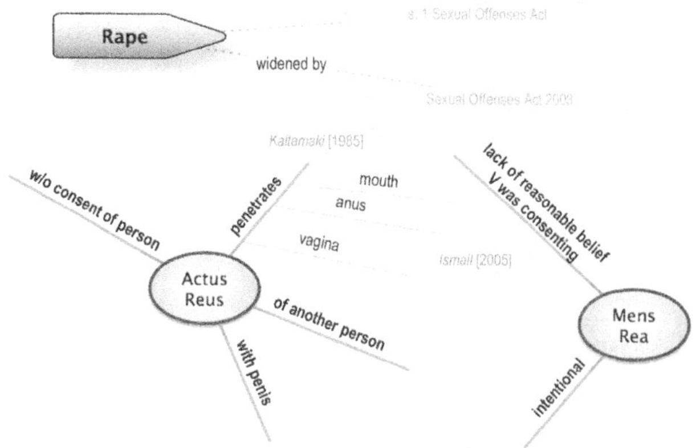


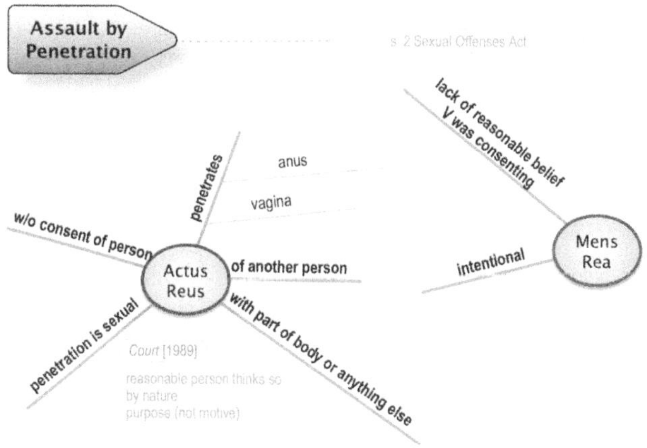

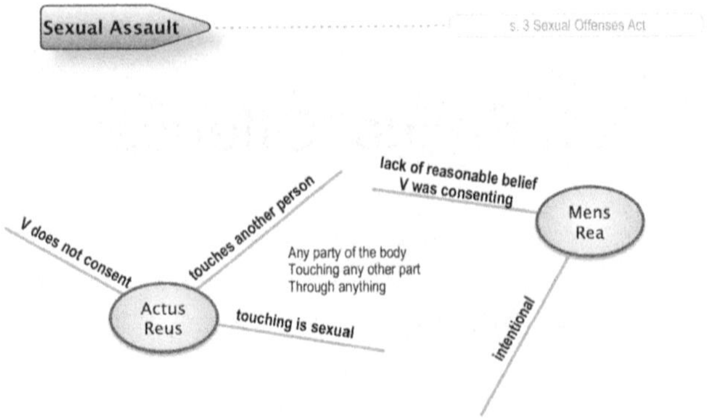
Sexual Assault
s. 3 Sexual Offenses Act
Actus Reus
V does not consent
touches another person
touching is sexual
Any party of the body
Touching any other part
Through anything
Mens Rea
lack of reasonable belief
V was consenting
intentional

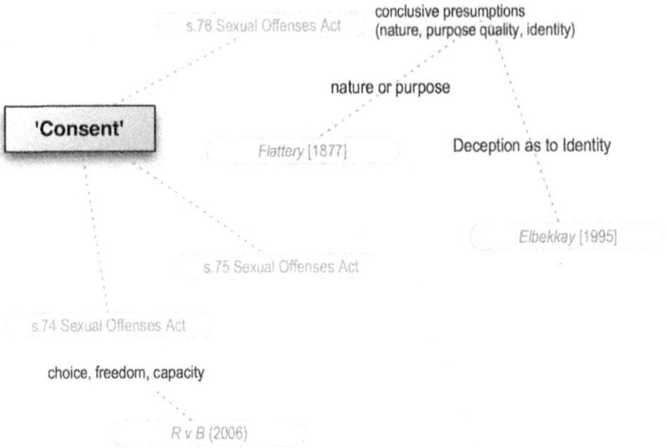
'Consent'
s.76 Sexual Offenses Act
conclusive presumptions
(nature, purpose quality, identity)
nature or purpose
Flattery [1877]
Deception as to Identity
Elbekkay [1995]
s.75 Sexual Offenses Act
s.74 Sexual Offenses Act
choice, freedom, capacity
R v B (2006)

# 12. Defenses 1: Failure of Proof and Justificatory Proof

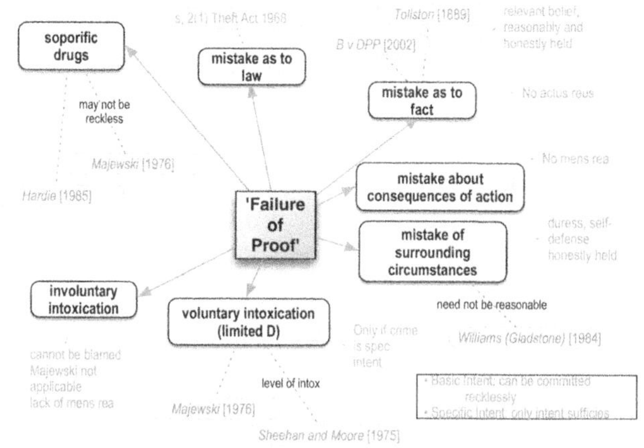


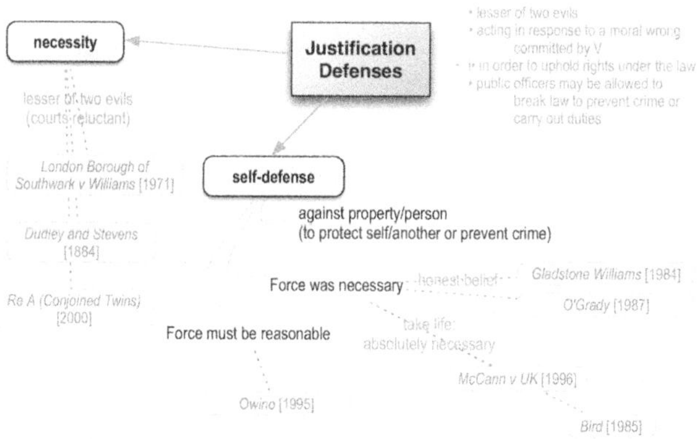

# 13. Defenses 2: Excusatory and Mental Disorder Defenses

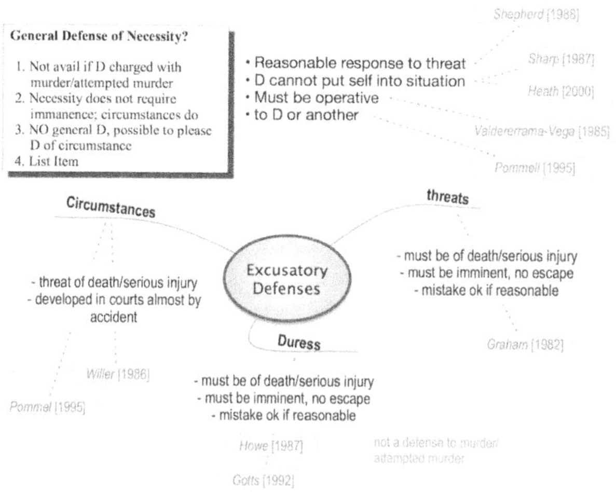


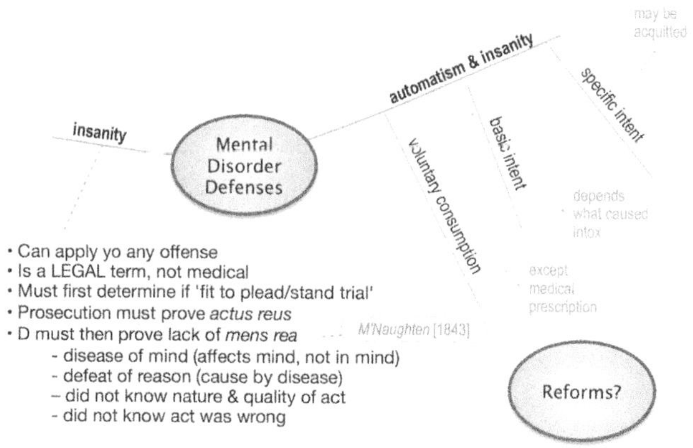

# 14. Attempt

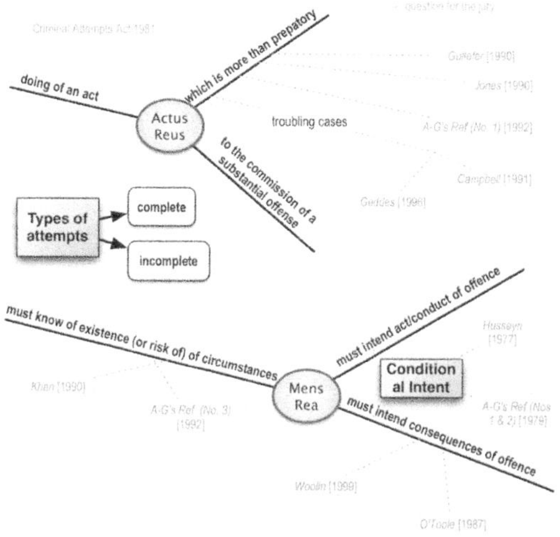
Criminal Attempts Act 1981
doing of an act
Actus Reus
which is more than prepatory
to the commission of a substantial offense
troubling cases
Jones [1990]
A-G's Ref (No. 1) [1992]
Campbell [1991]
Geddes [1996]
Types of attempts
complete
incomplete
must know of existence (or risk of) of circumstances
Khan [1990]
A-G's Ref (No. 3) [1992]
Mens Rea
must intend act/conduct of offence
Husseyn [1977]
Condition al Intent
A-G's Ref (Nos 1 & 2) [1979]
must intend consequences of offence
Woolin [1999]
O'Toole [1987]

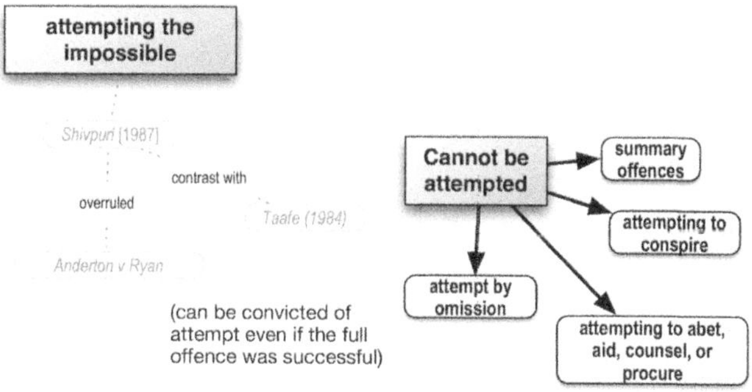
attempting the impossible
Shivpuri [1987]
overruled
Anderton v Ryan
contrast with
Taafe (1984)
(can be convicted of attempt even if the full offence was successful)
Cannot be attempted
summary offences
attempting to conspire
attempt by omission
attempting to abet, aid, counsel, or procure

# 15. Parties to Crime

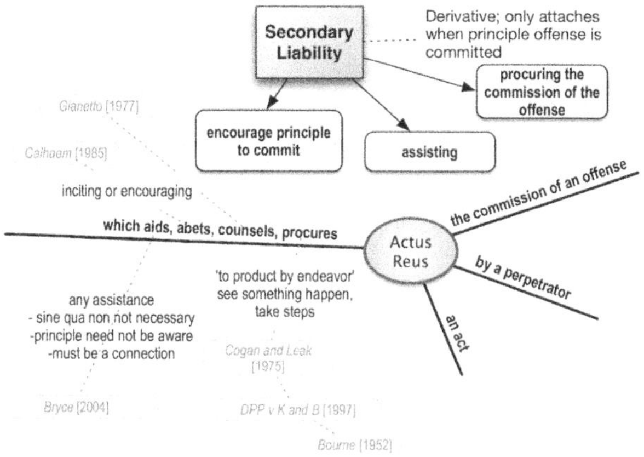


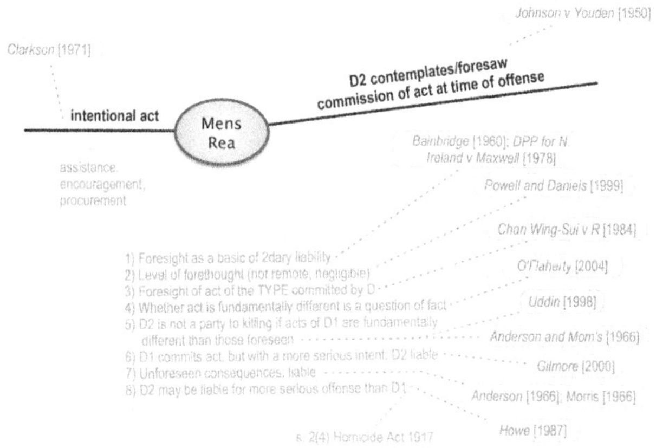

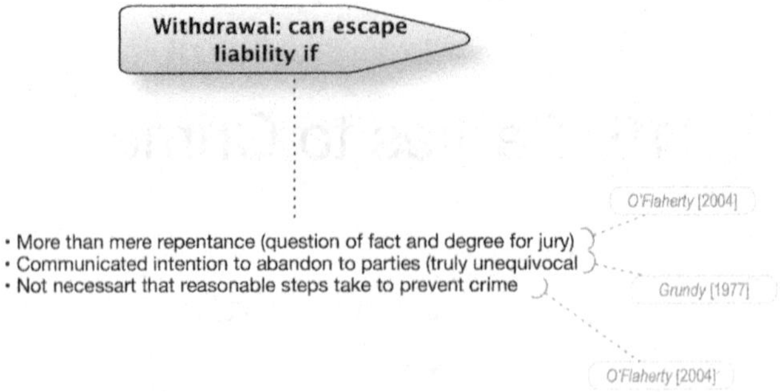
Withdrawal: can escape liability if
• More than mere repentance (question of fact and degree for jury)
• Communicated intention to abandon to parties (truly unequivocal
• Not necessart that reasonable steps take to prevent crime
O'Flaherty [2004]
Grundy [1977]
O'Flaherty [2004]

# 16. Theft and Fraud

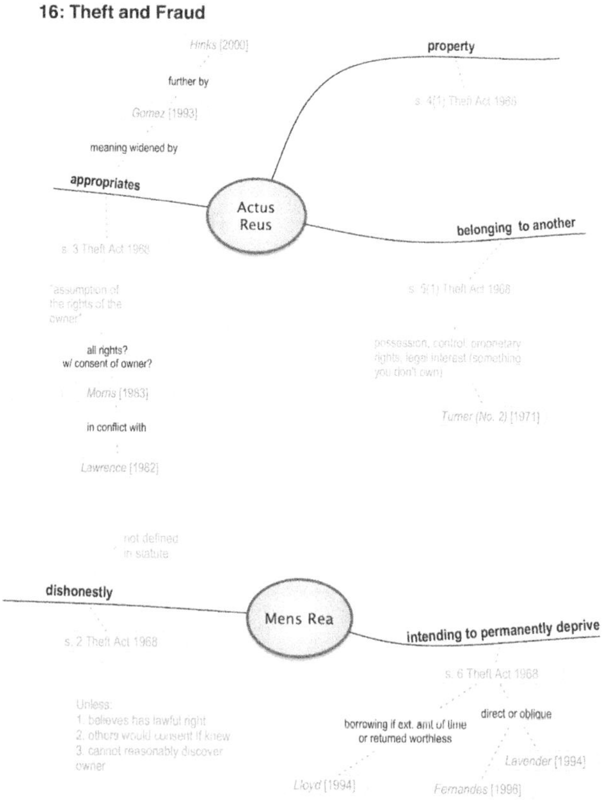

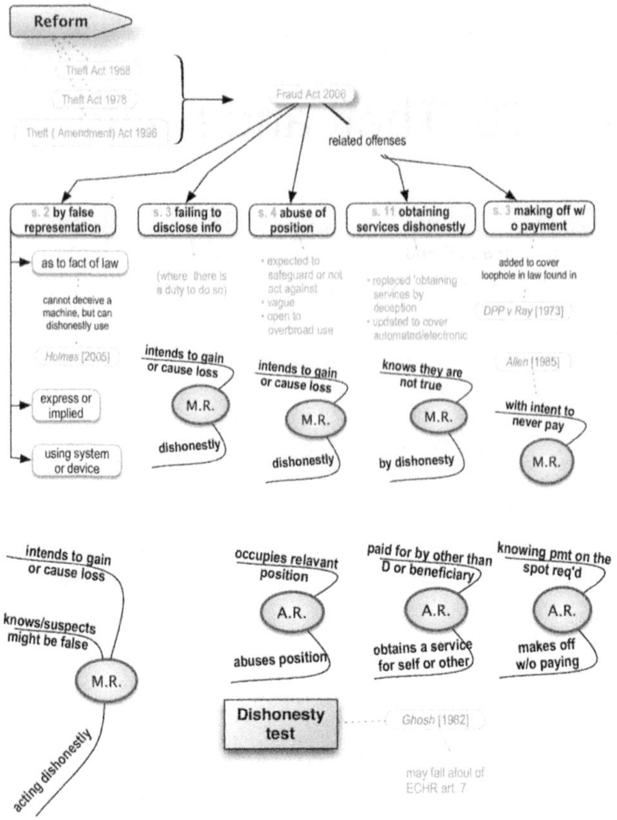
Reform
Theft Act 1968
Theft Act 1978
Theft ( Amendment) Act 1996
Fraud Act 2006
related offenses
s. 2 by false representation
s. 3 failing to disclose info
s. 4 abuse of position
s. 11 obtaining services dishonestly
s. 3 making off w/ o payment
as to fact of law
cannot deceive a machine, but can dishonestly use
Holmes [2005]
express or implied
using system or device
(where there is a duty to do so)
• expected to safeguard or not act against
• vague
• open to overbroad use
• replaced 'obtaining services by deception
• updated to cover automated/electronic
added to cover loophole in law found in
DPP v Ray [1973]
Allen [1985]
intends to gain or cause loss
M.R.
dishonestly
intends to gain or cause loss
M.R.
dishonestly
knows they are not true
M.R.
by dishonesty
with intent to never pay
M.R.
intends to gain or cause loss
knows/suspects might be false
M.R.
acting dishonestly
occupies relavant position
A.R.
abuses position
paid for by other than D or beneficiary
A.R.
obtains a service for self or other
knowing pmt on the spot req'd
A.R.
makes off w/o paying
Dishonesty test
Ghosh [1982]
may fail afoul of ECHR art. 7

# 17. Robbery

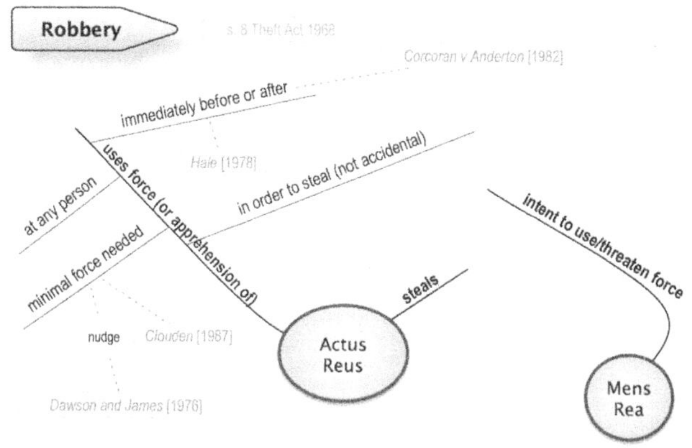

Robbery
s. 8 Theft Act 1968
Corcoran v Anderton [1982]
immediately before or after
Hale [1978]
uses force (or apprehension of)
in order to steal (not accidental)
at any person
minimal force needed
nudge
Clouden [1987]
Dawson and James [1976]
steals
Actus Reus
intent to use/threaten force
Mens Rea


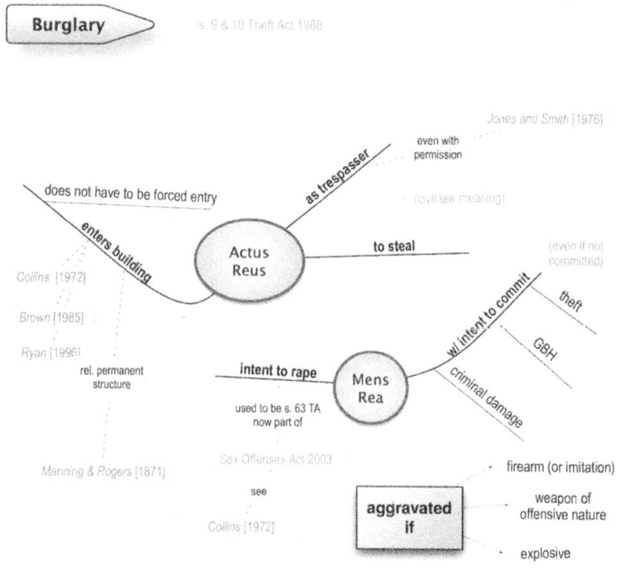

Burglary
s. 9 & 10 Theft Act 1968
Jones and Smith [1976]
even with permission
as trespasser
does not have to be forced entry
enters building
Actus Reus
to steal
(even if not committed)
Collins [1972]
Brown [1985]
Ryan [1996]
rel. permanent structure
Manning & Rogers [1871]
w/ intent to commit
theft
GBH
criminal damage
intent to rape
Mens Rea
used to be s. 63 TA now part of
Sex Offenses Act 2003
see
Collins [1972]
aggravated if
firearm (or imitation)
weapon of offensive nature
explosive

# 18. Criminal Damage

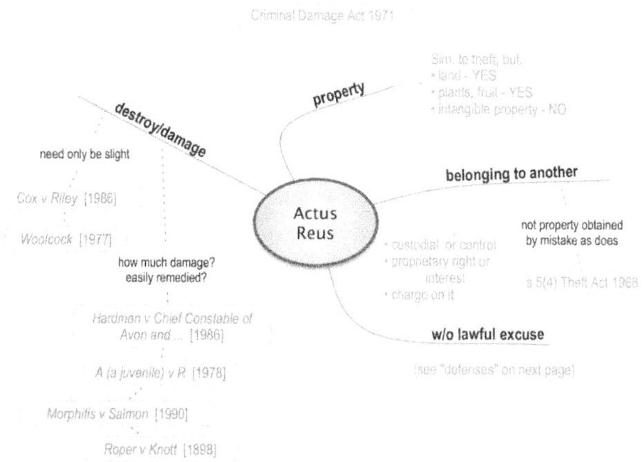


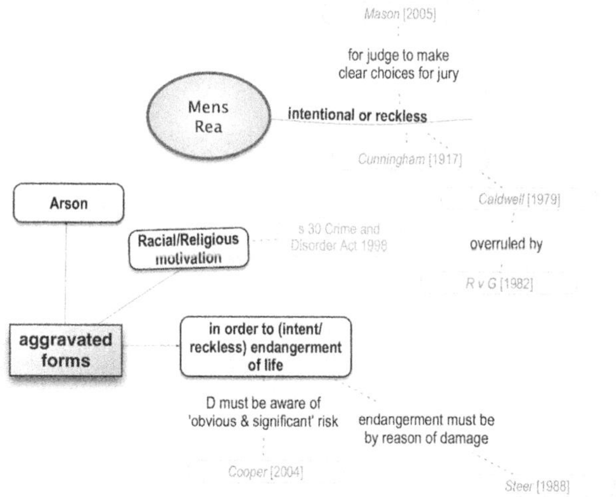

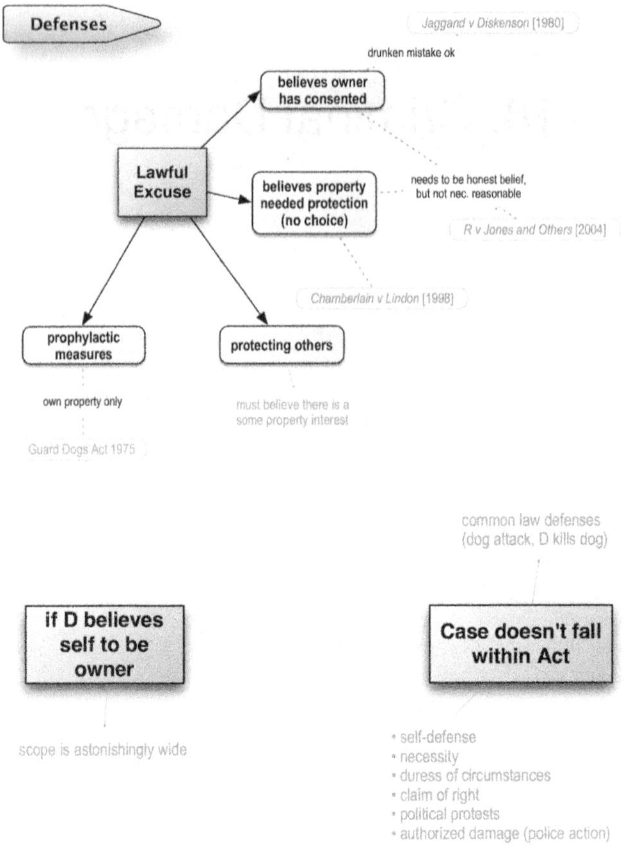
Defenses
Jaggand v Diskenson [1980]
drunken mistake ok
believes owner has consented
Lawful Excuse
believes property needed protection (no choice)
needs to be honest belief, but not nec. reasonable
R v Jones and Others [2004]
Chamberlain v Lindon [1998]
prophylactic measures
protecting others
own property only
must believe there is a some property interest
Guard Dogs Act 1975
common law defenses (dog attack, D kills dog)
if D believes self to be owner
Case doesn't fall within Act
scope is astonishingly wide
• self-defense
• necessity
• duress of circumstances
• claim of right
• political protests
• authorized damage (police action)

# Exam Study Sheets

# 1. Introduction

Exam Study Sheets are condensed outlines, based on the Course Outlines above. These are designed to help you "get the big picture" for revising and for testing yourself on the details. Each Crib Sheet contains 1–5 pages on each of the topics covered in the Course Outlines and Diagrams, including a few key statutes and cases for each. Suggested study plan.

1. Look over the readings, Course Outlines and Course Diagrams for the first topic.
2. Using the Crib Sheet for the first topic, test yourself on each item. Can you explain each one in detail? Can you remember important elements, discuss cases and statutes, and explain the concepts?
3. Review the Course outlines and Diagrams in areas where you are weak. Refer to your course materials to revise and review.
4. Repeat for each topic in the course.
   When you are preparing for your exams, use the VisuaLaw Crib Sheets as one of your tools for testing yourself.

# 2 Elements of an Offense

## 2.1In General

Statutory and Common Law offense involve

- Actus Reus
    - Mens Rea

Strict Liability

## 2.2 Proof

Burden on prosecution to prove BRD. Woolmington v DPP (1935)

Basic intent. Deller (1952)

## 2.3 Lawful Excuse

# 3 Actus Reus—Voluntariness

## 3.1 Prior Fault

- Non-Self-Induced automatism (blow to head, hypoglycaemia, swarm of bees in car): defense to specific and basic intent crimes (Sullivan — epileptic fit, has to protect society against a recurrance)
- Self-induced automatism = not a defense to basic intent crimes (self-intox as no D to BI applies to automatism (Majewski [1977])
- Non-dangerous drugs may provide defense to basic intent offenses
  Valium, committed arson (*Hardie* [1985])
  Insufficient food after insulin (*Bailey* [1983])

## 3.2 Insane Automatism (internal factor likely to occur, need not have suffered for any length of time)

- Special verdict (NGRI), mental hospital (mandatory until Criminal Procedure (Insanity and Unfitness to Plead) Act 1991 gave other options)
- If raised by D: BOP to prove on the balance of probabilities (Woolmington) — rare
- Raise by P: BOP BRD by M'Naughten Rules — often raised in response t o D raising sane automatism
- Disease of the mind: hyperglycaemia, sleepwalking, epilepsy
  3.3 Sane automatism
- a complete defense, caused by external factor (hypoglycaemia — Quick [1973]; concussion, alcohol, drugs)

– Can be negated by:
  Any control, trance-like state, purposive movements (*A-G's Reference (No. 2 of 1992)* [1993])
  Where it can be brought within the ambit of the rules of insanity
  (see below)
  Where there was prior fault (see below)

## 3.4 Background

– BOP on prosecution to show that D was guilty BRD with a voluntary act (Woolmington v DPP [1935]) (insanity is an exception: BOP is on D)

– Involuntary act not punishable (without control of mind, spasm, reflex, concussion, sleepwalking) (Bratty v A-G for NI [1961])

– Example: swarm of bees in car, malevolent passenger, blackout, vehicle failure (Bell [1985])

# 4. Actus Reus—Omissions

## 4.1 Duty to Act under Common Law

4.1.1 Under contract (Pittwood [1902])

4.1.2 Induced situation, became aware of it (Miller [1983])

4.1.3 Parent's duty, even if not blood relative (Gibbins and Proctor [1918])

4.1.4 Acceptance of care (Stone and Dobinson [1977])

## 4.2 Distinguishing between and Act and a Duty/

4.2.1 Medical treatment omission (Airdale NHS Trust v Bland [1933])

4.2.2 Medical treatment act (Re A (Conjoined Twins) [2001])

4.2.3 Lethal Injection (Cox [1992])

## 4.3 New Categories of Duty

4.3.1 Not duty for suppliers of drugs (Khan and Khan [1994])

4.3.2 Is duty a matter of law or fact? (Singh (Gurpal) [1999])

4.3.3 Except in unusual circumstances (doctor, parent), the question of whether a DoC exists is a question of fact for jury (Willoughby [2004])

4.3.4 Whether duty of care exists, Q of law for judge (Evans [2009])

## 4.4 Actus Reus - Circumstances element

4.4.1 Some crimes require the existence of specific circumstances as part of the AR (e.g, s.1(1) Criminal Damage Act 'property belonging to another'

4.4.2 Sometimes results in strange or unfair results (Larsonneur [1933])

# 5 Actus Reus—Consequences

## 5.1 Factual Causation

5.1.1 Determined by reference to the sine qua non

5.1.2 A necessary condition, but not the only one

5.1.3 Whether something is a factual cause of an event is for the jury

5.1.4 Courts assume that there can be causation by omission (Instan [1893])

## 5.2 Legal Causation

5.2.1 Judge directs whether something can be a legal cause; jury decides whether the facts make it so.

5.2.2 Expert evidence plays a role, but not determinative (see Jordan and Malcherek and Steel)

- Jordan criticized on these grounds; Smith described as unusual case on the facts
- Malcherek and Steel did not overrule Jordan, but distinguished it as exceptional

5.2.3 Must be operating, substantial, substantive, significant

- does not have to be main cause of death (Smith)
- Must be outside the de minimus range, have a bearing on the acceleration of death (Cato)

5.2.4 Result must be attributable to culpable act

- Dalloway [1847]; Campbell, Yateman, Henry [2009]
- Must take victims as they are found (Blaue [1975])

## 5.3 Intervening Causes

### 5.3.1 Once D starts chain of events, liable unless a novus actus interveniens (act of God, 3d party, act of V)

- Not reasonably foreseeable; causes the original act to no longer be 'operating and substantial' (see Pagett)

### 5.3.2 Escape Clause (D so frightened killed/injured trying to escape; unless 'so daft' will not break chain (William and Davis [1992])

### 5.3.3 Killing by Fright (Hayward; Watson)

### 5.3.4 Neglect by V

- Where D neglects to treat an injury inflicted by D, D likely held accountable (Dear)
- Palpably wrong medical interventions (Jordan —> Smith —> Malcherek and Steel)
- Unless negligent medical treatment so independent and potent that it makes D's acts insignificant (Cheshire)

# 6 Mens Rea

## 6.1 Introduction

### 6.1.1 Does not apply to crimes of negligence or strict liability

### 6.1.2 Motive is generally irrelevant, (i.e., mercy killing), but if purpose is to relieve pain, knowing it will hasten death, not mens rea (Adams; Airdale NHS Trust v Bland)

### 6.1.3 Mistaken belief may negate MR (difference between allowing to die and killing)

### 6.1.4 Basic Intent

- reckless is sufficient
- P must prove BRD that D was reckless and aware of risk (R v G)
- Self-intoxication is not a relevant defense

### 6.1.5 Specific Intent

- Recklessness will not suffice (sufficient for MS [BI crime] not murder [SI crime])
- Intention, purpose, aim (e.g, murder: intent to kill or cause GBH)
- Self-intoxication is a relevant defense

### 6.1.6 Ulterior Intent

- Commits a crime while intending to commit another
- Guilty of both basic MR (intent/recklessness) for the first, and ulterior intent if second (even if not actually committed)

- Ex: burglary is entering building as a trespasser with intent to commit other crimes; wounding with intent to cause GBH, wounding/GBH with intent to prevent/resist arrest

## 6.2 Intention

### 6.2.1 Direct Intent: purpose is to achieve a particular outcome

### 6.2.2 Oblique Intent: particular outcome is not primary intention, but should know it will happen based on actions

### 6.2.3 Important cases

- DPP v Smith; Hyam: went beyond ordinary meaning of 'intent' (criticized, no longer followed)
- Moloney, then Hancock and Shankland, then Nedrick: jury is to be directed that they can only infer intent if death/GBH was virtual certainty as result of actions (can find, do not have to)
- Woolin: substituted 'find' for 'infer'
- Matthews and Alleyne: CA confirmed Nedrick/Woollin, did not lay down a substantive rule of law; for death or really serious injury (maybe others?)

## 6.3 Recklessness

### 6.3.1 Unjustified risk-taking; deliberate and conscious when it is unreasonable to do so

### 6.3.2 Debate: should liability/punishment for recklessness be imposed for advertent/subjective recklessness AND for inadvertant/objective recklessness

- Originally had a subjective meaning (Cunningham)
- Then, D could be reckless even if not foreseen (Caldwell — much criticized)
- Overruled by R v G (Caldwell misinterpreted 'reckless' in Act): D is reckless where (1) in circumstance that D is aware risk is or will exists and (2) a result when D is ware of risk

## 6.4 Coincidences of AR and MR

6.4.1 Must coincide in time (Jakeman)

6.4.2 if AR can be a continuous activity, then MR must occur at some point during (Fagan v MPC)

6.4.3 Series of events as part of a plan can be enough (Thabo Meli), or even if no plan (Church)

6.4.4 See also Le Brun and A-G's Ref (No. 4 of 1980)

## 6.5 Transferred Malice

6.5.1 While doing an unlawful act with intent, if another unlawful even is committed, D is also guilty of second crime (Latimer)

- exception: not where AR achieved is not AR intended (A shoots B, misses, breaks window—no criminal damage

6.5.2 Transferred Malice is relevant to any of the defenses available

6.6 Negligence

6.6.1 Not really a MR term, but spoken of that way

6.6.2 Assessed objectively

6.6.3 Very few offenses of negligence: GNMS (Adomako); rape (lacks reasonable belief V was consenting)

## 6.7 Strict Liability

6.7.1 An offense in which one or more elements of AT need no MR or Negligence (must still be voluntary act)

6.7.2 Five principles to be considered when determining (Gammon v A-G of Hong Kong)

- presumption of MR
- Strong presumption where act is 'truly criminal'
- Presumption applies to statutes, only displaced if clear or necessary implication

- Can be displace where statute is concerned with issue of social concern, public safety
- Even where above is true, presumption stands unless creation of strict liability will encourage greater vigilante against commission

# 7 Murder and Manslaughter

## 7.1 Differences between Murder, Involuntary MS, and Voluntary MS

### 7.1.1 Murder: intention to kill or cause GBH

### 7.1.2 Involuntary MS

- Constructive MS: unintentionally & unforeseeably kills another while committing unlawful act which was likely to cause GBH
- GN MS: breach of Duty of Care which caused death, so serious to warrant criminal liability
- Reckless MS: deliberately taking unjustified risk causing serious injury

### 7.1.3 Voluntary MS

- Loss of Self Control: where killing results from qualifying trigger (replaced provocation, Coroner's and Justice Act 2009 s.54, 56)
- Diminished Responsibility: at time of killing, suffering from DR (new definition in Coroner's and Justice Act 2009 s.52)
- Suicide Pact: MS not murder (Homicide Act s.4)

## 7.2 Actus Reus of Murder and MS (Sir Edward Coke, 1552-1634)

### 7.2.1 Unlawfully (see Re A (conjoined twins))

### 7.2.2 Killeth

- Must be legal cause of death (not necessarily factual cause)
- Only necessary to show that act(s) accelerated death (Re A (Children))

- Medical definition of death considered in Malcherek; Steel; Airdale NHS Trust v Bland

### 7.2.3 Any Reasonable Creature in rerum natura

- Not murder to kill fetus in womb (A-G's Reference (No. 3 of 1994))

## 7.2.4 Within the Queen's Peace

## 7.3 Mens Rea of Murder

### 7.3.1 'malice aforethought' is misleading: 'intention to kill or cause GBH' (Maloney)

### 7.3.2 Intention (Woollin; applied in Matthews and Alleyne)

- if aim/purpose was to kill/GBH
- if not aim/purpose, but knew death/GBH was 'virtually certain', jury is entitled, but not obliged, to find intention
- if D foresaw risk of death/GBH, but at a lower level than 'virtual certainty,' this is not sufficient for intention

### 7.3.3 Intention to cause GBH

- Intention to cause GBH suffices for murder (Cunningham)
- Much academic and judicial criticism (Daniels and Powell; English)

### 7.3.4 Recent case: Mount

## 7.4 Constructive MS (Involuntary MS by Unlawful and Dangerous Act)

### 7.4.1 D performed an unlawful act

- Negligent offense not enough, must be act with mens rea (Andrews)
- Civil wrong insufficient (Franklin)
- Omission insufficient (Lowe)

– Prosecution must prove all elements of the crime (Cato; DPP v Newbury); better approach is Lamb.

### 7.4.2 The unlawful act was dangerous ('if all sober and reasonable people...' Church)

### 7.4.3 The unlawful act was the legal cause of death

## 7.5 MS and the Administration of Drugs

### 7.5.1 If D injects another, even with consent, liable (Cato)

### 7.5.2 Self-injection

– Act of supply not directed at V, not liable (Dalby)

– later cases held that unlawful act need not be aimed at V (Mitchell; Goodfellow; A-G's Ref (No. 3 of 1994))

– Preparer of syringe guilty as secondary (Kennedy [1999]; how can there be secondary without principle?)

– Kennedy flawed, but in some cases supplier might be guilty of MS as principle (Dias)

– D held tourniquet while V injected; active participation; widened definition of 'administered' (Rogers)

– Jury to decide whether D caused substance to be administered; not necessary to prove actions were sole and immediate charge (Finlay)

– Finlay, Rodgers wrongly decided; when a person freely and deliberately injects self supplier is not liable for act or consequences (Kennedy (No. 2))

## 7.6 MS by GN

### 7.6.1 Modern approach requires high degree of proof for negligence: such disregard for life and safety that it amounts to crime against the State (Bateman); some found unsatisfactory,

shifted from from expressing fault as recklessness (Stone and Dobinson; Seymour)

### 7.6.2 HL thought too rigid, switched back to Bateman in Adomako

- D owed a DoC
- Breach of duty amounted to GN (objective question for jury)
- Breach of DoC caused death (no need to prove D foresaw risk of death (A-G's Ref (No. 2 of 1999))

### 7.6.3 Critique

- circular (seriousness of breach of duty; so much so that it risked death; if so, then it was a serious breach...)
- law is uncertain
- jury required to decide issue of law
- liability for serious offense should not be based on objective fault (R v G)

### 7.6.4 Answer to Critiques (Misra)

- There is an element of circularity, but it does not result in uncertainty which offends against Art 7 ECHR
- There is some uncertain, juries may vary, but this is acceptable—otherwise the law would be too rigid
- They are not required to decide issue of law; comments in Adomako about law to to merely insure the jury took into account the need or gross negligence.
- R v G only addressed recklessness as to Criminal Damage

### 7.6.5 Duty of Care

- A matter for the jury unless formal (doctor/patient, etc.) (Willoughby)
- unforeseen results not liable (Lewin); deliberate act, liable (Ruffell)

– Must take reasonable steps (Evans)

## 7.7 Reckless MS

7.7.1 Anyone who kills, having foreseen serious risk of death/ GBH, takes it without justification (Hyam)

7.7.2 Foresight, in absence of intention to kill/GBH, no longer suffices for murder (but does for MS)

# 8 Defenses—Voluntary Manslaughter

## 8.1 Loss of Control

### 8.1.1 Partial defense (Murder to MS) replaces partial defense of Provocation (Coroner's and Justice Act 2009) (no appeals as of Feb 2011)

### 8.1.2 Loss of Self Control

- not necessary to lose complete control (Richens)
- Need not be sudden (Duffy)
- Delayed reaction okay, but must be attributable to provocation (Ahluwalia)
- Controversy: gender differences, isn't 'loss of self-control' always sudden?; cannot be for revenge?

### 8.1.3 Must be result of Qualifying Trigger

- Fear of Serious Violence (where D overreacted, does not have to be reasonable fear; against D or other person)
- Justifiable sense of Being Wronged (limited to extremely grave things—assumed to be objective)
- Combined triggers (both of above)
- Limitations: if incited by D for excuse; sexual infidelity

### 8.1.4 Evaluations

- Objective: sex, age, with normal degree of tolerance/self-restraint for such a person
- Short temper, etc., may not be taken into account, but history of abuse can

- If a mental disorder played a role, reduced liability from murder to MS possible

## 8.2 Diminished Responsibility

### 8.2.1 Statutory defense applying only to murder (principles and secondaries, but not for attempt) (Campbell) (Homicide Act 1957)

### 8.2.2 Burden of Proof

- If D pleads, BOP (s.2(2); Dunbar)
- If D pleads insanity, P can raise Diminished Responsibility BRD (Criminal Procedure Insanity Act s.6; Grant)
- Plea can be accepted by judge where medical evidence is undisputed (Cox)

### 8.2.3 Elements of Defense

- Abnormality of Mental Functioning Arising From Recognized Medical Condition (pychoses, mood disorders, neuroses, conditions (dementia, epilepsy), battered woman syndrome, morbid jealousy)

*Medical evidence: availability is question for jury, if nothing casts doubt, must accept it (*Dix; Walker)

- Substantial Impairment of Specific Abilities in respect to ability to (1) understand nature of conduct similar to M'Naughten Rules (2) form a rational judgement (3) exercise self-control
- Abnormality Explains D's Act/Omission in killing (need not be sole cause, but must be significant factor)
- Related to Insanity: Insanity limited to diseases 'all or nothing'; DR requires substantial impairment, a matter of judgement and degree

### 8.2.4 Alcohol, Drugs, and Diminished Responsibility

- Transient effects do not constitute abnormality of mind (Di Duca)

- fact of intoxication does not prevent defense if it would have been successful without (see Hill under old law—prob the same)
- Alcohol Dependency Syndrome: recognized medical condition (Tandy); depends on juries findings as to nature and extend of syndrome (Stewart)

# 9 Assault, Battery, Defense of Consent

## 9.1 Common Assault

### 9.1.1 A&B are gateway offenses, not serious

### 9.1.2 No proof of harm needed

### 9.1.3 Offenses against the Person Act (no definition, just penalties

- s.20: Malicious wounding or inflicting GBH (more serious than A&B)
- s.18: Wounding or causing GBH with intent (even more serious)

### 9.1.4 Criminal Justice Act 1988 (no definition, just stated

summary offense and penalty)

## 9.2 Assault

### 9.2.1 Actus Reus

- cause another
- to apprehend
- immediate (need not be instantaneous (Smith v Chief Superintendent of Woking Police Station); Constanza)
- unlawful
- violence (need not be hostile, rude, or aggressive, V need not be afraid; only apprehend it.

### 9.2.2 Mens Rea

- Intention or recklessness (intended to cause, or was aware of risk); recklessness is subjective (Pros must prove BRD that D foresaw risk of causing V to apprehend...)

### 9.2.3 Words Might negate (Turberville v Savage)

### 9.2.4 Words alone, even silence, might be enough (Ireland, Burstow)

## 9.3 Battery

### 9.3.1 Actus Reus

- Infliction (No battery by omission; Fagan v MPC; DPP v Santa Burmudez)
- Immediate
- unlawful
- violence (ordinary touching in course of life not enough: must be hostile; Wilson v Pringle)

### 9.3.2 Mens Rea

- Intention or recklessness (intended to cause, or was aware of risk); recklessness is subjective (Pros must prove BRD that D foresaw risk of causing V to apprehend...)

## 9.4 Consent as a Defense

### 9.4.1 Limits: must be specific, but can be implied (holding arm out, being jostled in crowd)

### 9.4.2 Consent must be real

- Fraud negates defense (Tassebaum; Flattery), but must go to nature of act (Konzani, R v B)
- Duress may negate, may be implied from relationship
- Capacity

### 9.4.3 Even true consent may be negated on public policy grounds

- Consenting fistfight where more than transient or trifling (AG Ref (No. 6 of 1980)
- Caning of 17-year-old girl with consent for sexual gratification (Donovan)
- Sado-Masochism (Brown; approved in A-G Ref (No. 6 of 1980)).
- Bodily Mutilation (within limits ok, ear-piercing of children, but not cheek mutilation)
- Sports (ok if reasonably to be expected)

# 10 Assault Occasioning Actual Bodily Harm

## 10.1 Assault occasioning actual Bodily Harm (Offences Against the Person Act 1861 s47)

### 10.1.1 Not a new offense, but see Courtie [1984]

### 10.1.2 Actus Reus

- pychiatric injury. Chan Frook [1994]
- Not transient or trifling. Miller [1954]
- Cutting hair without consent. DPP v Smith [2006]

### 10.1.3 Mens Rea

- Savage and Parmenter (1991)

## 10.2 Malicious Wounding or Inflicting GBH (Offences Against the Person Act 1861 s20)

### 10.2.1 Actus Reus

- Different from bodily harm in degree. Saunders [1985]
- Wound, not a scratch. Moriarty v Brooks **(1834)**
- psychiatric abuse enough. Burstow (1997)

### 10.2.2 Mens Rea

- Requires proof that the D was aware conduct carried risk of some harm, albeit not serious — s.20; Savage and Parmenter approving Mowatt [1967]

## 10.3 Racial or Religious Aggravation (Crime and Disorder Act 1988 s29)

### 10.3.1 If at the time of a crime, or immediately before or after

### 10.3.2 Wide view of race or racial group. DPP v M [2004]; see R v Rogers [2007]

## 10.4 Wounding or Causing GBH with Intent and Malicious Wounding with Intent to Resist or Prevent Arrest (Offences Against the Person Act 1861 s.18)

### 10.4.1 Malicious wounding with intent

### 10.4.2 Causing grievous bodily harm

### 10.4.3 Actus Reus

– Same as wounding and GBH

– Mandair [1995]

### 10.4.4 Mens Rea

– offenses often charge in alternatives

R v Hadson (Danielle) [2009]; Morrison [1989]; R v Gregory (Matthew) [2009]

# 11 Sexual Offenses

## 11.1 Law Reform Process

### 11.1.1 Sexual Offenses Act 1956 amended in 1994 and 2000 brought male rape and marital rape into definition

### 11.1.2 2000 began process of reforming law (Setting the Boundaries consultation paper)

### 11.1.3 2002 White Paper, Protecting the Public

### 11.1.4 Resulted in Sexual Offenses Act 2003

## 11.2 Rape (max penalty: widened offense more than previous) (s.1)

### 11.2.1 Actus Reus

- Penetration of vagina, anus, mouth — a continuing act (Kaitamaki); no presumption one worse than the other (Ismail)
- with penis
- V does not consent
- (removed 'unlawful,' marital rape now included (R v R)

### 11.2.2 Mens Rea

- Intentional penetration
- lack of Reasonable Belief that V consented (objective—must be honest and reasonable; jury may take into account age, mental capacity, previous relationship)

## 11.3 Assault by Penetration (new offense, deliberate overlap with Rape) (s.2)

### 11.3.1 Actus Reus

- Penetrates vagina or anus
- With part of body or anything else (both D and V can be man, woman, transgender)
- V does not consent
- Penetration is Sexual (if reasonable people would think so) (Court)
- Purpose, not motive (as in all criminal offenses)

### 11.3.2 Mens Rea

- Intentional Penetration
- lacks Reasonable Belief V consented (objective—must be honest and reasonable; jury may take into account age, mental capacity, previous relationship)

## 11.4 Consent

### 11.4.1 Prosecution must show that V did not consent AND D did not reasonable believe V consented

### 11.4.2 s.76 – Conclusive Presumptions (not rebuttable)

- Deceit as to Nature of Act (Flattery)
- includes purpose/quality of act (SOA goes further than common law by adding quality: knows act is sexual, but deceived as to why —purpose enough, no causal link needed (Tassebaum — Quality; Green — Purpose; see Jheeta for definition of 'purpose')
- Deceit as to Identity: confirms common law position in Elbekkay (someone personally known) — must be causal link, not invalidate consent unless deceit goes to nature/purpose (Richardson) (faking dentist not enough, sex for tooth repair would be)

### 11.4.3 s.75 — Evidential Presumptions (rebuttable)

- Consent presumed to be invalid if violence (threat, actual, fear of); V detained/D not; V asleep/unconscious; physically disabled (but not mentally); D causes V to take substances which stupifies

### 11.4.4 s.74 —General Consent

- Agrees by choice, has freedom and capacity to do so
- wide definition, long list of examples
- time frame matters, though
- HIV case (R v B)

# 12 Defenses 1

## 12.1 Failure of Proof—Mistake

12.1.1 As to Law: ignorance no excuse, exceptions; theft b/c truly believed he was owner (Theft Act 1968)

12.1.2 As to Fact: must be honestly held, need not be reasonable (Tolson)

12.1.3 As to Surrounding Circumstances: honestly held, not necessarily reasonable (William (Gladstone))

12.1.4 Drunken Mistakes: does not apply when mistake was induced by drunkenness (O'Grady)

12.1.5 Mistakes relating to Mens Rea: honest but mistaken belief negates MR, same for intent (R v G)

- does not apply to sexual offenses: consent must be honestly AND reasonably held

## 12.2 Failure of Proof—Intoxication

### 12.2.1 Limited defense

- because MR may not be there through fault of D; Majewski tried to find legal solution)
- First must determine if D is drunk enough to consider defense (based on lack of MR)

### 12.2.2 Voluntary Intoxication

- Only a defense if crime is specific intent (Majewski)
- Led to much criticism for lack of legal reasoning and accuracy, breaches principle of continuity (compare Thabo Meli, Fagan, with Cunningham)

### 12.2.3 Involuntary Intoxication

- lacks MR, makes no difference if basic or specific intent crime (Majewski does not apply)
- However, if offense requires no MR, then no defense
- Soporific drugs: even if causes unusual aggression, may not be reckless under Majewski; see Hardie, Bailey)

## 12.3 Justificatory Defenses

### 12.3.1 Self-Defense

- Sources: Criminal Law Act 1967 (permits reasonable force in arrest/stopping crime) Owino (honestly believes force needed; used reasonable force); Criminal Justice and Immigration Act 2008 (complex attempt to clarify reasonable); Criminal Damage Act 1971 (if honestly believed necessary to protect property)
- Force Used Must Be Necessary: subjective (William (Gladstone)); cannot provoke (Brown); preemptive okay if reasonable (Beckford)
- Force used Must Be Reasonable (Owino)
- Cannot be used to reduce a charge: all or nothing (might be able to plead loss of control to reduce)

### 12.3.2 Necessity (Lesser of Two Evils)

- Courts usually reluctant to allow (London Borough of Southwark v Williams; Dudley and Stevens)
- It is no general defense except in exceptional circumstances
- May be available at CL where: (1) best interest of a patient (2) D has statutory duty to act (police) (3) exceptional cases such as Re A.

# 13 Defenses 2

## 13.1 Excusatory Defenses

### 13.1.1 Duress (a complete defense)

- Not a defense to murder (Howe) or attempted murder (Gotts)
- pressure involving serious threat of death/GBH which compels D to act unlawfully
- does not have to be physical, 'will was overborne'
- Courts expect highest degree of heroism (Howe)

### 13.1.2 Threats

- Can be against other people (Martin)
- D must believe it will be carried out if he does not commit crime; must be the threat which compels act
- Cannot put self in position to be threatened (i.e., join a gang, Sharp; Shepherd)
- Mistake as to threat okay, if mistake is reasonable ((A-G's Ref (No. 2 of 1999)))
- No avenue of escape ((A-G's Ref (No. 2 of 1999)))
- Reasonable response taking into account characteristics of D (Bowen)

### 13.1.3 Circumstances

- developed through a series of road cases (Conway; Harris)
- Does not apply to murder/attempted murder (Pommell)
- Probably no general defense of necessity

## 13.2 Mental Disorder Defenses

### 13.2.1 Insanity

- a denial of MR; can apply to any defense; is a legal term (not medical — Sullivan)
- D must first be judged 'fit to stand trial' (Antoine)
- Prosecution must prove AR, no need for MR; D then proves lack of MR through M'Naughten Rules
- Elements: disease of mind; defect of reason; did not know nature/quality of act; did not know what he was doing was wrong

### 13.2.2 Sane Automatism

- Outcome: acquittal
- Only succeeds where lack of control is from external source AND there is no control over actions (A-G's Ref (No. 2 of 1992))

### 13.2.3 Automatism and Intoxication

- Voluntary consumption of non-prescriptions drugs
- Courts have applied Majewski rules (specific intent, may be acquitted; basic intent, depends on what caused intox)

### 13.2.4 Reform

- antiquated definition of 'disease of mind)
- Law Commission Draft Criminal Code 1989 proposed alternative terms

# 14 Attempt

## 14.1 Actus reus

14.1.1 Complete and incomplete. Gullefer [1990]; Jones (1990); Attorney-General's Reference (No. 1 of 1992) [1992]

14.1.2 Hard cases: Campbell [1991]; Geddes [1996]

## 14.2 Mens Rea

14.2.1 meaning of 'intent'. O'Toole [1987]

14.2.2 Conditional intent. Husseyn (1977); Attorney-General's Reference (Nos 1 and 2 of 1979) [1980]

14.2.3 D muster know existence of circumstances or risk thereof. Khan [1990]; see Law Commission (Law Com No 318 (2009))

## 14.3 Attempting the impossible

14.3.1 Criminal Attempts Act 1981 s.1(2)

14.3.2 Shivpuri [1987]; Taafe [1984]

14.3.3 Offenses which cannot be attempted

14.3.4 Can be convicted of attempt even if successful

# 15 Parties to Crime

## 15.1 Secondary Liability

### 15.1.1 Accessories and Abettors Act 1861

### 15.1.2 Terminology — Bryce [2004]

### 15.1.3 Mode of participation. Attorney General's Reference (No. 1 of 1975) [1975]; Howe [1987]

### 15.1.4 Only derivative

## 15.2 Actus Reus

### 15.2.1 Aid

### 15.2.2 Abet or counsel. Calhaem [1985]

### 15.2.3 Procuring. Attorney General's Reference (No. 1 of 1975)

### 15.2.4 Can apply even if first D not guilty. Cogan and Leak

[1975]; DPP v K and B [1997]; Bourne [1952]

## 15.3 Mens Rea

### 15.3.1 Act of assistance is intentional. Clarkson [1971]

### 15.3.2 At time of act, D2 foresaw the commission of offense by D1. NCB v Gamble (1959); Bainbridge [1960]; Hyde and Others (1991);

### 15.3.3 Level of foresight required. Miah (Aziz) [2009]

### 15.3.4 Foresight of the type of act committed. English [1997]; Greatrex [1999]

- Fundamentally different. Uddin [1998]; Anderson and Morris [1966]

- Foreseen, but eventually a more serious intent. Gilmour [2000]; Roberts, Day and Day [2001]; Attorney General's reference (No. 3 of 2004) [2005]
- Liability for unforeseen consequences. Anderson; Morris [1966]
- D2 may be liable for more serious offense than D1. Homicide Act 1957 s.2(4)

## 15.4 Withdrawal

15.4.1 Before act is committed or reached stage of attempt. Grundy [1977]

15.4.2 Generally must be an act (question of fact for jury). O'Flaherty [2004]

15.4.3 Must communicate the withdrawal. Mitchell and King (1998); Rafferty [2007]

15.4.4 Liable for actions before withdrawal. Rafferty; Campbell [2009]

# 16 Theft and Fraud

## 16.1 Theft

### 16.1.1 Actus Reus

- Appropriation (most controversial)
  any, if not all rights (*Morris* [1983])
- Consent relates to dishonesty, not appropriation (*Lawrence* [1972])
- Act does not say that authorization/consent could *never* amount
  to appropriation (*Gomez* [1993])
- Consent irrelevant (*Hinks* [2000])
- Property
  money, real or personal property, things in action
  not land, but rights to land; not animals unless in captivity not picking flowers/fruit unless for commercial purposes
- Belonging to another (possession, control, proprietary right)
  can own property without knowing it (*Woodman* [1974])
  Golf course owns lost balls on it (*Hibbert v McKiernan* [1948])
  Can steal something you own (*Turner (No. 2)* [1971], compare *Meredith* [1973])

### 16.1.2 Mens Rea

- Dishonesty (Act provides examples: honestly held, need not be reasonable)
- Act provides examples: honestly held, need not be reasonable (right in law, owner would consent, cannot discover owner reasonably)

*Ghosh* [1982] test: (1) objective—dishonest to reasonable person, (2) subjective—did D realize, by those standards, action was dishonest?

- Intention to permenantly deprive to treat thing as own, dispose of, borrow/lending might be (*Lloyd* [1985])
    - 'dispose of' does not necessarily mean literally throw away

(*Lavender* [1994])

- deal with in a manner that D knows he is risking its loss

(*Fernandes* [1996])

## 16.2 Fraud

### 16.2.1 Reform

- Theft Act 1968: obtaining property by deception, pecuniary advantage
- Theft Act 1978 added obtaining services by deception, evading liability by deception
- Theft (Amendment) Act 1996 added obtaining money transfer by deception
- Law Commission review 2002 addressed problems if IDing what had been obtained, whether deception caused it; updated for modern situations
- Resulted in Fraud Act 2006

### 16.2.2 Fraud by False Representation (broad new offense)

- as to fact, law, or state of mind
- express or implied (words, omission, behavior) [DPP v Ray; Charles; Gilmartin; Lambie]
- using a system or device (old Acts: could not deceive a machine)
- Causation: does not need to actually cause a loss (intent suffices), V does not have to be deceived (criminalizes lying!)

- Mens Rea
  knows it might be false or misleading
  Intends to make gain or cause loss for self or another (no recklessness—if jury finds foresight as to gain/loss virtually certain, can find intent (*Woolin*) [excludes land and non-pecuniary gains)
  acting dishonestly

### 16.2.3 Fraud by Failure to Disclose Information

- legal duty to disclose (from statute, contract, trade/market custom, agent/principle relationship, etc.)

### 16.2.4 Fraud by Abuse of Position (vague)

- trustee/beneficiary, director/company, professional person/client, employee/employer, within family, etc.
- Need not intend loss, but by other, for a gain

### 16.2.5 Obtaining Services Dishonestly

- replaced old offense of obtaining services by deception
- service itself is obtained, not monetary value (free services not covered)

### 16.2.6 Making Off Without Payment

- Does not require deception (closed loophold discovered in DPP v Ray)
- Need not be by stealth (Brooks and Brooks)
- No need to ID exact 'spot' (Aziz); payment need not be at 'spot' if other arrangements made (Vincent)
- Must intend to never pay, not just pay later (Allen)

# 17 Robbery and Burglary

## 17.1 Robbery (Theft Act 1968 s.8)

### 17.1.1 Actus Reus

- Stealing. Corcoran v Anderton (1980)
- Force
- Can be minimal. *Dawson and James* (1976); *Clouden* [1987]

Need not be directed at owner
Must be at time or before act. Hale (1978)

### 17.1.2 Mens Rea

- Theft Act 1968 is silent to mens rea
- Dishonest intent to permanently deprive. Skivington (1968); Robinson (1977)

## 17.2 Burglary (Theft Act 1968 s.9-10)

### 17.2.1 Entering a building as a Trespasser

- Enter. Collins [1972]; Brown (1985); Ryan (1996)
- Building. Royal Exchange Theatre Trust v The Commissioners [1978]; Manning and Rogers [1871];
- Trespasser. Jones and Smith [1976]

### 17.2.2 Three ways act can be committed.

- Section 9(1)(a)-(b) intent or actual commission. Jenkins **(1983)**
- With intent to commit sexual offense. Sexual Offenses Act s. 63
- Aggravated with firearm, weapon of offense (Williams (1977)), explosive (Francis (1982); O'Leary (1986).

# 18 Criminal Damage

## 18.1 Actus Reus

### 18.1.1 Destroy (demolish, kill, spray weedkiller on favorite plant...)

### 18.1.2 Damage — need be only slight (scratching a car, cracking a window)

- *Cox v Riley, Hardman v Chief Constable of Avon) Woolcock)*
- Property — Criminal Damage Act 1971 s.10(1)

### 18.1.3 Belonging to Another

## 18.2 Mens Rea

### 18.2.1 Intentional

### 18.2.2 Reckless

- *R v G* (prior: *Cunningham* and *Caldwell*)

## 18.3 Aggravated Criminal Damages

### 18.3.1 Actus Reus: same

### 18.3.2 Mens Rea: same, but must also be proved D was aware of obvious and significant risk of danger to life (Cooper following R v G on appeal)

## 18.4 Arson

### 18.4.1 two possible counts:

- Arson with intent to endanger life
- Being reckless as to whether life would be endangered

#### 18.4.2 Requirement to charge with arson also meant

*Drayton*

## 18.5 Defenses

#### 18.5.1 Basic intent crime, self-induced intoxication is no defense (Majewski)

#### 18.5.2 If D has a genuine belief that property is his, not guilty (Smith)

#### 18.5.3 Lawful Excuse

– BOP on prosecution

– Criminal Damage Act s.5(2)

– *Jones, Chamberlain v Lindon*

- *Hunt, Wang*

# About the Authors

Duncan Brown holds a law degree from the University of London, and is an information technology consultant. He is the webmaster and a writer for Legal Yankee, a website of resources for law students in the UK and the US.

Jessica Patel is a freelance paralegal, graphic designer, and writer. She is a staff writer and researcher for Legal Yankee, a website of resources for law students in the UK and the US.

Made in the USA
Monee, IL
08 November 2026

68116179R00125